Helping the Living and the Dying

To this day I live in three worlds and have learned to enjoy it tremendously. The only place I have found where these three worlds connect is in a hospice, which is where I spend time with people who are dying. It is there that people nearing the ends of their lives make a connection with the spirit world. By being with dying people, I am able to share in their world as they pass over to the other side. As they transfer to their spiritual side, they are actually living in two worlds at the same time. A person who does hospice work lives in those worlds with the dying.

It is in hospice work that a person can realize that death is not feared.

In the early days, I had no understanding about what was happening. I knew only that I had no control over the things that were coming into my mind.

In looking back I realize that my experience was like flying an airplane without first being given lessons. I was bound to crash, and crash I did.

Until I finally earned my wings.

Books by Dannion Brinkley with Paul Perry

Saved by the Light
At Peace in the Light

Published by HarperPaperbacks

ATTENTION: ORGANIZATIONS AND CORPORATIONS

Most HarperPaperbacks are available at special quantity discounts
for bulk purchases for sales promotions, premiums, or fund-raising.
For information, please call or write:
Special Markets Department, HarperCollins*Publishers*,
10 East 53rd Street, New York, N.Y. 10022.
Telephone: (212) 207-7528. Fax: (212) 207-7222.

HarperSpotlight

AT PEACE IN THE LIGHT

The Further Adventures
of a Reluctant Psychic Who Reveals the
Secret of Your Spiritual Powers

DANNION BRINKLEY

WITH PAUL PERRY

HarperPaperbacks
A Division of HarperCollinsPublishers

HarperPaperbacks A Division of HarperCollinsPublishers
10 E 53rd Street, New York, N.Y. 10022

A hardcover edition of this book was published in 1995 by
HarperCollins*Publishers*.

Cover photograph by Michael Britto

First HarperPaperbacks printing: August 1996

Printed in the United States of America

HarperPaperbacks, HarperSpotlight, and colophon are
trademarks of HarperCollins*Publishers*

❖10 9 8 7 6 5 4 3 2 1

*This book is dedicated
to the Baby Boomers:
As we are having to face
our own Mortality.
And to help those who we Love
and who have Loved us face theirs!!
May we face our lives with
grace in these times.*

Contents

Acknowledgments

THERE ARE DOZENS OF PEOPLE who deserve acknowledgment for this book, many of whom I want to mention here. My co-author, Paul Perry, our editor, Diane Reverand, and our agent, Nat Sobel, truly made this book happen.

For Melanie Hill, who kept it all working; Jan Dudley, for her insight; Joanne Hartley, for always being there when I need her; and Valerie Vickens, for the music. And to all the hundreds of hospital and hospice workers and patients in transition I have met in the last twenty years.

And to the most important one of all, my dad.

Foreword

I FIRST MET DANNION BRINKLEY while waiting for a car to arrive at the Omni Hotel in Chicago. We were both scheduled to make an appearance on the *Oprah* show and the guests were all instructed to meet in the lobby and ride over to Harpo Productions together.

As my wife, Sallie, and I exited the elevator and began to meet the other participants, a booming voice interrupted from the rear, "Jimmy Red, I've been wanting to meet you. We Southern boys got to stick together."

Looking up, I watched a large man with soft eyes walking toward us. He smiled widely and pulled us into a huge, enveloping Dannion Brinkley hug, which he dispensed to the other guests as well. Later, although Oprah never knew, the best show occurred in the Green Room backstage, where Thomas Moore and Marlo Morgan joined us for a lively discussion of everything from the trials of publishing to conspiracy theories.

For Dannion and me the conversation has never ended, taking place either by telephone, often across continents, or at Hawkview, our place in Alabama. And what I have discovered about Dannion is that as incredible as it may seem, he is exactly the person he appears to be.

Yes, he used to be an intelligence operative, a background that caused him much agony in his first near-death life review, but which prepared him well for the kind of global-military-economic-cultural analysis that rolls off his tongue as easily as the Southern drawl and good ol' boy attitude he picked up during his upbringing in South Carolina.

And yes, he is one of the most gifted psychics that I have ever met, leaving a constant trail of stunned believers in his wake. "The first time I spoke on the phone with him," my editor once told me, "he named everything that was on my desk, described my office exactly, and then took me on a mental tour down the hall, describing my co-workers and all the office politics that no one could possibly have known about."

But, for Dannion, all this ability and humor is precisely focused on an urgent sense of mission. (When I last spoke with him, for instance, he had been in thirty-two presentations in the last ninety days, while also giving interviews, lecturing, and teaching classes in hospice techniques.) When I asked him why he followed such a torturous schedule, he told me he felt he could make a difference if he could have an impact on society in just one area: health care, and especially alternative health care, for the final days of life when the most money in traditional medicine is spent in an often cruel extension of existence for a few hours or days.

His main theme is this: If we can dispel our fear of death, we can dispel our fear of life, our fear of living up to our fullest, most spiritual potential. Key to ending fear, he believes, is training people to help make the transition to death a loving, gentle, and normal experience. The people at several hospice associations tell me that he has already recruited more hospice volunteers than anyone in their histories.

My own opinion, however, is that Dannion's contribution is even wider than that, for in spite of the fact that he is often loud and boisterous and casts into the trees too much when fishing, the man is a model. Here in the 1990s, we are moving from a theoretical understanding of spirituality to actually living what we know, which can be very difficult. Somehow we have to understand and follow our intuitions, stay connected with our sense of mission, discern how and when to intervene in people's lives, and, above all, portray ourselves honestly to others whether they are skeptical or not.

In this, Dannion has no equal. He spends much of his time on a variety of talk shows, bantering with professional debunkers, and he never retreats for a moment. "You only have to kill me a couple of times and I get the message," he is fond of saying. "We are great and powerful spiritual beings. And we're all beginning to realize it."

Dannion Brinkley's lasting contribution is that he does realize it, and he wears it outwardly for all the world to see.

JAMES REDFIELD

Chapter 1

STALKED
BY THE LIGHT

A person who has a cat by the tail knows a whole lot more about cats than someone who has just read about them.

—MARK TWAIN

Since being struck by lightning in 1975, I have had a special ear for thunder. As far as I am concerned, every storm is a stalker, every bolt of lightning is a possible killer. I can't help thinking of lightning that way. Even the roll of distant thunder makes me uneasy, filling me with painful memories and uncertainty. "I liked being dead, because it felt so alive," I have often said. "I just didn't like using lightning to get there."

On a summer day in 1994, I almost became a victim of lightning again, without even knowing it was close to me.

At Peace in the Light

It happened at a time of peace for me. I had just returned from five months of lectures and publicity for my first book, *Saved by the Light,* and finally I had a chance to be alone. In order to savor this quiet time, I went to house-sit at a friend's farm near my home in South Carolina.

On this particular day, I had brought with me a box of letters from people who had read the book. For the first time in months, I planned to be alone and do nothing but read and relax.

As I put my feet up on the couch, I noticed that a gentle rain had begun to fall outside. The weather set a relaxing mood, and before long I was dozing off to the rhythm of the rain.

Then the telephone began to ring. It brought me out of a deep sleep and into a fog of semiconsciousness. Had it rung three times? Four? I didn't care. Whoever it was could wait. This wasn't my house, anyway. I decided to just let it ring.

As I started to go back to sleep, I noticed that the rain had begun to fall so hard that it nearly drowned out the phone's ring. *Tough day for the toads,* I thought. And then it happened. A flash of lightning sizzled in the room, accompanied by a cannon shot of thunder. The telephone ring stopped—dead.

Again? I thought. Suddenly I was upright on the couch, perspiration from this jolt of fear beginning to dampen my shirt. I could smell the burned air and could even taste its acidic flavor as I began to pant for the oxygen that my frightened heart demanded.

Stalked by the Light

I stood slowly and walked across the room. The telephone was on the floor. *Where did it hit?* I wondered.

As I scanned the room I could see that nothing looked damaged. I looked out the window at the telephone box. Its door was sprung open and steam was rushing out.

I swallowed hard.

It happened again, I thought, returning to the sofa. *Am I ready?*

I sat down slowly and pondered what had just occurred. I closed my eyes and let my mind run backward. Without having to die this time, I envisioned vivid details about my life.

I thought about the precious things in my life. My mother and the rest of my family immediately came to mind. I considered all the personal trials we had weathered, yet we had managed to remain friends. I thought about the strange journey that my near-death experience had started me on, and the many people I had touched with my story. My mind ran backward through my search for meaning until it reached 1975 and the date of my phone call from God.

I now remembered the moment of that strike vividly. With my heart pounding, I slipped so deeply into myself that I shut out the world around me. Inside my mind, I relived the event that had changed my life as though it were happening again.

*I*n my mind it was September 17, 1975, the day on which my life was forever changed. I was twenty-five years old, in the best physical shape of my life. It was seven at night, and in the next moment I would be dead.

Outside I could see lightning streak across the sky, making that sizzling sound before it popped.

"Artillery from God," someone in my family had called it. Over the years I had heard dozens of stories about people and animals being struck and killed by lightning. As scary as ghost stories were to me, the lightning stories my great-uncle would tell at night when the summer storms rumbled and the room would fry with bright flashes were even more terrifying. That fear of lightning had never left me. I wanted to get off the telephone quickly.

"Hey, Tommy, I've got to get going, a storm's coming."

"So what?" he said.

Just having returned from a trip to South America only a few days earlier, I had to take care of some business matters. As the rain fell outside, I was finishing one more phone call to a business partner before getting off the telephone. "Remember, if you get a phone call from God, you have a good chance of becoming the burning bush," I think my great-uncle said, but I am sure he meant it as a joke.

"Tommy, I gotta go. Mother always told me never to talk on the phone during a thunderstorm."

"What's the matter, tough guy, do you always do what your momma tells you?" he asked.

And that was it. The next sound I heard was like a freight train coming into my ear at the speed of light. Jolts of electricity coursed through my body, and every cell of my being felt as if it had been bathed in battery acid. The nails of my shoes were welded to the nails in the floor so that when I was raised into the air my feet were pulled out of them. I saw the ceiling in front of my face, and for a moment I could not imagine what power it was that could cause such searing pain and hold me in its grip, suspended over my own bed.

Somewhere down the hall my wife, Sandy, had shouted, "That was a close one," when she saw the lightning and heard the thunder. But I didn't hear her say that, I only found out about it much later. I also didn't see the horrified look on her face as she peered down the hall and saw me stretched out, blasted above the bed. For a moment all I saw was the plaster of the ceiling, when the lightning threw me into the air.

Probably at that point my heart stopped. Sandy began giving me CPR and soon Tommy showed up. He had been a corpsman in the navy and knew all there was to know about lifesaving techniques. The two of them worked me over until the ambulance arrived and then rode with my body to the hospital. I rode with my body too. As the ambulance sped through the rainy streets, I was out-of-body and watching the scene as though I were a part of it, yet not a part. I could see myself lying there as Sandy wept. The attendants did what little they could to bring life back to my body. Then I heard the attendant say, "He's gone," as the race to the hospital continued.

At Peace in the Light

While the doctors and nurses tried to jump-start my heart, I went up a tunnel that spiraled around me and vibrated with the sound of heavenly chimes.

The tunnel that engulfed me was dark, but ahead was a light that became brighter and brighter as I moved toward it. Soon I was in a paradise of brilliant light, a soothing illumination that bathed me in a love and comfort that made me feel as though I were as weightless as helium and as loved as a newborn child.

As this happened, a shimmering silver form appeared. It came like a silhouette through the fog. As it approached I felt a deep sense of love that became so intense that it was almost too pleasurable to withstand. I looked at my hands and the rest of my body. I could see that I had become translucent and shimmering, like water in a coral sea or a scarf made of fine silk blowing in a gentle breeze.

The Being of Light that stood in front of me was magnificent. It looked as though it was composed of thousands of tiny diamonds, each glowing with the colors of the rainbow. I didn't know if it was male or female, only that it was great and powerful, yet gentle.

As I admired the Being's beauty I was engulfed, and every memory flowed from my mind as though a dam had broken and all the water had spilled out. In a great rush my life flowed past me and I was able to see it all, the good, the bad, the ugly, and the beautiful.

*M*y twenty-eight minutes of death included all the emotions in the universe. With the spirit guide

I visited a crystal city and received visions of the future from thirteen Beings of Light. They gave me 117 predictions, many of which have come true.

They revealed to me changes in the earth as well as changes in the way the government sees itself. They showed me the rise and fall of different countries in the Middle East and how those shifts in power would occur. They also gave me a preview of the coming struggle in Western culture over health care, as well as the economic collapse of the dollar and the decline of the cities. They showed me an array of good things as well. Information about medicine was made clear to me, for instance, that revealed a positive future. They made it clear to me that if we do not recapture our spirits, we will not be able to cope with the future.

They told me how to create Centers where people could find their spiritual selves through stress reduction. They told me that it would be my mission on earth to create them. They let me experience a taste of spiritual perfection and then they sent me back to my mortal body, which was singed from the inside out by 180,000 volts of lightning.

Millions of people have described similar experiences while near death. Whether struck down by lightning or a heart attack, or badly damaged by the trauma of an automobile accident, millions have had near-death experiences and lived to tell about a visit to the spiritual realm.

They arrive in this place the same way I did. They leave their bodies and go up a tunnel. At the end of this tunnel they encounter Beings of Light. They also encounter themselves in an event that researchers call the panoramic life review. To their amazement, their entire lives unfold before them. During this event, they see their whole lives and the effect they have had on everyone they have encountered. This life review is where you learn that "do unto others as you would have them do unto you" is not just a philosophy, but a law.

The life-review portion of the near-death experience is, I believe, the greatest agent for change. At some points the reflections from this review are quite painful. For example, when I was in elementary school I sneaked up behind one of my classmates and pulled the rug he was standing on out from underneath him. The move took him completely by surprise, and he slammed face first against the concrete. When he rolled over and sat up, he was bleeding from the mouth. On the ground where he had landed were his two front teeth. There was no pain in his face as he gazed at me, just a look of dazed astonishment as he wondered what had happened.

I saw that boy's face again in my life review, along with the entire incident. This time, however, I experienced it from his side as well. I felt the painful surprise of being slammed to the ground with no warning and even looked back as the boy did to see my grinning face. I could also tell in this life review why he didn't yell or cry after that happened. The wind had been knocked out of him by the impact. There was no air left in him to have any kind of response come out of his mouth.

In another reflection, I witnessed myself taunting a little girl, one of my classmates, as she walked to school. I could feel the power in my actions as I frightened the girl by threatening to hit her with a stick. At the same time, though, I could feel her fear. I tried to stop myself in the event that I was observing, but of course I was unable to do that. This was a life review, and the event I was reviewing had actually happened and could not be changed, only reflected upon.

My life review did not consist entirely of painful reminiscences. Some of them were pleasant to relive, and taught me that in the end, love is the most important thing there is.

In one astounding scene, I saw myself talking to a man at my father's store. I barely knew this person, but I could tell that he was deeply angry about something that had happened.

"What's wrong?" I asked him.

He began telling me about his teenaged son, and how the boy did not seem to care about anything. "He won't do his homework, and all he does when he is around me is try to start fights."

"It's just hormones," I said. "Tell him you love him and then leave him alone. He needs to feel wanted, but he feels crowded at the same time."

We talked for a while longer and then the man went back home. I relived this in the life review, only this time I was able to follow him home and see how my advice had affected his relationship with his son.

The man did what we had talked about, and before long his relationship with his son was better. Although this seemed like an insignificant event, I was able to see the chain reaction of change that can take place from any encounter, great or small.

Another portion of my life review came to mind that showed me how love can come in many forms. I had lied to my mother about something, and I could feel the sharp sting of the belt that she brought down on my rear end as she impressed upon me the importance of telling her the truth.

The whipping hurt me both physically and emotionally. The amazing thing, however, was how much it hurt my mother. In my life review I could feel the pain she felt as she spanked me. I could also tell that she was spanking me out of love so that I would grow up to become a better person.

Those who, like me, have had near-death experiences, especially ones with powerful life reviews, are never the same again. They lie in hospital beds and ask themselves the question that can be answered only through faith: "What happened when I was dead? What just went on? What did it mean?"

So it was with me in the days after the lightning strike. Did I really see my life pass before me in full review? I wondered. As nurses stuck me with needles and doctors whispered in the hall that there was no way I could still be alive, I lay in bed and wondered if I had truly been to a heavenly realm where cities glowed like crystal and beautiful spirits could impart information about the future. *What was that?* I thought. *What really did happen?*

Since then I have received all the proof I need that I stood in the presence of powerful spiritual beings during those twenty-eight minutes. Now I jokingly refer to the lightning strike as "the phone call from God." Back in those days, though, I was baffled by what had happened. . . .

I was roused from my reflections by the fury of the surprise storm. First came a torrent of water that beat hard against the roof. Then came more lightning in thin bolts that licked the green farmland. Their bright departure was followed immediately by the thunder, its deep bass rolling like the sound of a drum. For several minutes the air was so charged with electricity that I feared I might once again be struck by lightning. Always so close . . .

Are the Spirit Beings coming back for me? I wondered. *Are they looking for me again? And if they are, am I ready?*

Out of the fear came a thought: *A moment like this can be an opportunity instead of a curse.* I decided to seize the moment. Rather than allow myself to be steeped in fear, I decided to relive the last twenty years, to examine the events in my life that had convinced me we are all powerful spiritual beings. Had I found peace in the light?

I closed my eyes and relaxed. My mind flipped backward through nearly two decades until I found myself standing before thirteen Beings of Light. This was during the time that my heart had stopped, and for all intents and purposes I was dead. But the Spirit Beings knew better. They were filling me up with information to take back to the mortal world.

One by one they showed me glimpses of the future, 117 events in all, that would not begin unfolding for two and one-half years after I hobbled back to life from this world beyond.

I have never fully understood why they gave me the opportunity to see future events. Perhaps it was a way of keeping me on course. By seeing these future events and watching them unfold, I would never be able to walk away from the mission they had given me. Maybe I needed that constant motivation to keep me true to their goals.

Whatever the reason, the things that they showed and told me have come true over the years. I vividly remember my excitement as the silver-blue Beings stood before me and a box the size of a videotape came from their chests. As I was there in the crystal cathedral, the boxes zoomed right at my face and gave me puzzling and unforgettable visions of the future.

For example, one of the boxes revealed a terrifying vision of nuclear destruction. As clearly as though I were watching television, I could see hundreds of people dying in a beautiful forested area near a river.

The year that was given to me was 1986, and with it the word *wormwood.*

It wasn't until a decade later that I was able to associate those pictures in my mind with the explosion of the Chernobyl nuclear plant near Kiev in the Soviet Union. I made the connection because the meltdown took place in 1986, and also because Chernobyl means "wormwood" in Ukrainian.

They showed me a second nuclear accident that would take place in 1995 and was more subtle and sinister than Chernobyl. I saw tons of nuclear waste being secretly dumped in the ocean off the coast of Norway. The waste was put into five dump sites that had been chosen by high-level government officials in the former Soviet Union. After a few years, the waste began to leak.

Such an accident actually did take place in February 1995, long after it was revealed in my first book, *Saved by the Light.*

I was contacted by a number of readers in Europe who told me that the Russians had "disposed" of an old nuclear submarine off the coast of Norway. This submarine had begun leaking nuclear substances, which had been detected by government monitoring posts and were now being reported in the press.

I have received a number of letters and telephone calls from people all over the world referring to this Russian nuclear submarine that was dumped in the waters off Norway. Is this the second nuclear accident that the Beings of Light told me about? I am inclined to think that it is.

In 1975 the Spirit Beings showed me the collapse of the Soviet Union and told me that it would take place in 1989. Much of this collapse was due to the Chernobyl nuclear accident. What little trust in government the Russian people had was destroyed by that disaster. This nuclear problem, when heaped upon the other social and economic problems of the Soviet Union, led to its breakup.

This disintegration of the USSR was shown to me in a collage of images that included people carrying bags of money into stores and coming out with small bags of goods. I was shown military men wandering the streets and begging, obviously with no place to go. People ate rotten apples and rioted to get food from trucks filled with food. I watched the Mafia operating freely in a city that I thought was Moscow, and could tell that they had no fear of arrest. All of this has come true.

As I saw this, one of the Beings of Light said: "Watch the Soviet Union. How the Russian people go, so goes the world. What happens to Russia is the basis for everything that will happen to the economy of the free world."

To this day, Dr. Raymond Moody, the father of near-death studies, tells people how he thought I was a "madman" for telling him about this prediction for many years. I even went so far as to tell him that I would be in the Soviet Union with someone I knew when it fell apart. I told him this at the time of the Cold War, when the Soviet Union was an enemy of the United States. At that time, it was extremely difficult to arrange travel visas for Russia. Yet, during the fall of the Soviet Union, with its food riots and economic collapse, we were watching the catastrophe together on television. In 1992, Raymond and I were together in Moscow, where we watched people lining up and waiting for food.

I remember Raymond's look of surprise as he looked at me and said, "This is it! This is the vision you saw in the box!"

I saw events that came true after many of these prophecies were published in *Saved by the Light*. For instance, I was told of submarines that would come into the possession of Iran in 1993. I could tell that their purpose was to stop the shipping of oil from the Middle East. The crews of these submarines prayed frequently on their knees, and I sensed that this was some kind of religious mission.

Within six months of the book's publication, a

secret report was released showing that Iran had purchased three Kilo-class submarines from Russia and rocket boats from China.

The purpose of these subs, said Secretary of Defense William Perry, was most likely to control the passage of ships through the Strait of Hormuz.

"We are watching them [the submarines] closely, very closely," Perry told the *Washington Times*. "We follow these submarines very carefully, and I do get reports on them all the time."

I saw many scenes that were not of war, including visions of natural and economic disasters. These disasters led to millions of refugees streaming across the U.S. border, looking for a new life in North America.

There seemed to be nothing we could do to prevent these millions of people from leaving homelands like El Salvador and Nicaragua and crossing our lengthy southern border.

As a result of this exodus, Mexico's economy would be broken and ours would be strained. I said that this would happen by the year 2000 and would be triggered by the rise of socialism in Central America. This form of socialism would be deeply rooted in organized religion.

My co-author pointed to the North American Free Trade Agreement as a sign that this prophecy was not likely to take place. The collapse of the Mexican economy in early 1995 demonstrates that NAFTA is not as solid a proposition as some may have hoped. The next five years will tell.

One of the Beings of Light revealed to me that the events I had seen were the future as it now stood. He also told me that the future was not necessarily cast in stone. "The flow of human events can be changed, but first people have to know what they are," said the Being.

"The events will tell us, or we will tell them. Now that the future is known, it can be changed."

"Your role in the earth's existence is truly that of a hero," one of the Beings conveyed to me, referring to mankind. "Those who go to earth are heroes and heroines, because you are doing something that no other spiritual beings have the courage to do. You have gone to earth to co-create with God."

Co-create with God. What better definition of spirituality could I have? After giving me the glimpse of the future, the Spirit Beings even let me know exactly what I was supposed to do to co-create with God. They showed me how to create clinics they called "Centers." Through the use of a variety of equipment and specific programs, I was to create an environment of relaxation and stress relief. In such an environment, people could explore their spiritual selves while reducing stress in their everyday lives.

"Show people how they can rely on their spiritual selves instead of entirely upon the government and institutions," said one of the Beings. "Religions are fine, but don't let them replace spirituality. You must remember that you are a mighty spiritual being with tremendous skill and capability. All you need to realize is that love is powerful. Its expression is treating others the way they want to be treated."

Both of these—the prophecies and The Centers—have had a profound effect upon my life. However, these communications were not all I had to convince me that what had happened during my near-death experiences were real.

There were other things, strange things, that began to happen within a day or two after my heart started again. Those experiences convinced me that I had made contact with a different reality, or that it had made contact with me.

Chapter 2

WHAT IS
HAPPENING HERE?

*T*he first time it happened, I didn't recognize it for what it was. How could I? I had just been struck by lightning, and my days were filled with chaos and confusion. I could hear doctors say, "He probably isn't going to make it." Yet when I opened my eyes there was nobody in the room. Family members smiled and said, "You look wonderful," but they emitted their deeper thoughts. I could hear these thoughts, the gist of which was, "God, you look like a dead man."

What is happening here? I thought. The only answer I had was, *I don't know.*

The date was somewhere after September 17, 1975. The place was a hospital room in Augusta, Georgia. I was not only fighting for my life, but I was deeply confused. *Where had I gone when my heart stopped? Who were those thirteen spirits, and what was the meaning of the information they had given me?*

Even as I struggled for breath, the information played back in my mind over and over again. I now describe it as being like super memory, because it happened when I was dead. It played back with such persistence and intensity that those events seemed to occupy every part of my mind that wasn't already awash in pain. Whenever I closed my eyes or drifted off to sleep, I could sense and hear the Spirit Beings from the time when I was dead. They were showing me things from the future that made no sense to me in the present. They were telling me how to help mankind and prepare for what was to come through what they called "Centers." They were showing me how to build them. They were giving me a mission that would direct me for the rest of my life, sometimes driving me and everyone around me crazy.

When I opened my eyes, other disturbing things were happening. These were strange times indeed.

At first the events around me seemed to be a replay. It was as though everything I was experiencing had already happened and I was seeing it for a second time. I remember a friend coming into the room and saying that I didn't look bad for someone who had just been hit with 180,000 volts.

"Weren't you just here a minute ago?" I asked.

"No," he insisted. "I just got here."

That's funny, I thought. "I am sure I heard you say that already," I said.

"That's because you've been rewired," he said.

Experiences like that kept happening. Once I woke up to find a nurse in the room. I was sure she had been talking to me about her husband

and saying things that weren't very nice. I spoke up immediately.

"Just leave him," I said.

She looked at me for a moment and began to rub her chin. "How did you know what I was thinking about?"

Another time a new doctor came in and asked if he could examine my eyes. I was sure he had asked me that question already, and I told him to quit repeating himself. "Sir," he said angrily, "I haven't said enough to you to repeat myself yet."

These experiences happened again and again, sometimes with humbling results. For instance, an acquaintance named Scotty came to see me. He had heard that I had been struck by lightning and had come to see for himself just how badly off I was.

I remember lying flat on my back and staring at the ceiling. I could hear Scotty slip quietly into the room and place his hand on my foot. It was a touch of compassion, one that let me know he was genuinely concerned. What happened next filled me with fear. Since he had touched me, I could hear the conversations of others as they had talked to Scotty earlier that day about my condition. What they had to say was upsetting to me. As they talked about the accident, someone said sarcastically that it couldn't have happened to a nicer guy.

"Who cares, he got what he deserved," I heard a voice say.

"They don't think he's going to live, and I hope they're right," said another voice.

"Too bad the lightning bolt wasn't bigger," said someone else.

Could he possibly be talking about me? I wondered. *Was I really that bad?*

Some of the voices were familiar to me. Who they were did not concern me then. What disturbed me was that I was literally living inside people. As they came into the room, I was hearing their thoughts. If they touched me, I seemed to have a direct connection into their minds. Sometimes these thoughts were mixed with conversations they were having with others. If they told me something that wasn't true, I would hear their true thoughts. Often, I even heard conversations they had with others.

I couldn't figure out how this was happening, nor did I care. There was enormous pain in these early days. The lightning that had struck me in the back of the neck had essentially fried me from the inside out. The medical records say that I had "contusions of the spine." Whatever the medical terms were, all I really cared about was somehow catching my next breath and trying to find a place in my dreamlike reality that didn't have pain.

Regardless of what I cared about, I continued to hear them just the same.

What I heard was sometimes embarrassing.

A fellow I did business with came into the room with his wife. I was asleep, so he touched my leg to wake me up. In that brief instant, I could have sworn that he told me that he and his wife had gotten a divorce. "I never got along with her very well anyway," I heard him say.

When I opened my eyes, both he and his wife were standing there. I was startled. "I thought you guys got divorced," I blurted out.

"Why would you think that, Dannion?" asked the woman. "We're like an old pair of shoes. We'll never find another match."

A few weeks later she told him that she no longer felt compatible with him and that she wanted a divorce. The person who told me about it laughed.

"I guess you never can tell," he said. "I thought those two people were welded together."

Then another dimension was added to the déjà vu experience. It became visual.

It first occurred when an older woman named Mrs. Dawson came to see me. I knew this woman only in passing. She was the mother of a friend of mine. She was a gentle person. She came into the room and pulled a chair over to the side of the bed. As we talked she held my hand, and when she did that I was suddenly able to see pomegranates sitting on a living-room table. It was like a painting. I could see the rich brown wood grain in the table and sitting on top of it were three succulent pieces of fruit.

I couldn't figure it out. It was almost as though I were sitting right there in her home. I began to scan the room with my mind's eye. Then I looked out the window and saw a beautiful pomegranate tree. At the base of the trunk was a basket in which picked fruit had been piled.

"You've been picking pomegranates today," I said.

She glanced around the room and then gave me a surprised look. "How did you know that?" she asked.

I could only shrug because I honestly didn't know.

*A*nother time three nurses loaded me into a wheelchair and took me to the hospital's therapeutic whirlpool bath. This was a stainless steel tub filled with hot water that was circulated through nozzles. I was looking forward to this because it felt good to move in the warm water after long periods of bed rest.

When all three of them put their hands on me and lowered me into the whirlpool, I began to see a hodgepodge of images. I could tell that one of the women was thinking about her teenage son. As she moved my arm through the warm water, I could see her arguing with her son about going to college. One of the other nurses was helping me kick my legs. From her I could feel the love she had for a new boyfriend, and I could see the two of them sitting in a restaurant having a meal and enjoying one another's company. The third one had her hands under my back. She was engaged in a conversation with the other two nurses about work, but her mind was on other things. She had been arguing with her brother-in-law about a car that he had sold her and her husband. Even though she was laughing here in the therapy room, she was deeply angry with her relative over the car.

As I bubbled in this stainless steel hot tub, I realized that my mind had somehow tapped into a stew of pictures and thoughts from those who touched me.

What was going on? People came into my hospital room to wish me well and tell me how great I looked. It didn't take a psychic to know that they were lying. I could see them grimace in horror as they looked at the wreck that I had become. It is humorous now to remember how their words didn't match their reactions. "You look great, Dannion," said one woman whose face became as pale as a sheet. A couple of friends looked faint, and one nearly threw up when he saw the condition I was in.

The way these people reacted to me made what was on their minds obvious. Still, something was happening that was not so obvious. When someone visited in a truly emotional state, I could feel that emotion and then I could hear his thoughts. I was not just analyzing them, the thoughts were being conveyed to me. I could feel compassion even if the people visiting didn't wear it on their faces. I could also feel the coldness of people who came to see how I was doing and acted warmly toward me.

One time I just walked into a person's life without even knowing what I was doing.

A woman visited with a friend of mine. She was from out of town, and I knew nothing about her. These two just stopped by for a few moments on their way to a movie.

When I touched her hand, I could see in my mind a handsome man with gray hair who was about twenty years older than she. I saw this in the way that many people can see a memory, like a home movie. Only I was not seeing my memory, but that of the woman whom I had just met. As I saw the two of them talking in a nicely appointed room, I could tell exactly how she felt about him.

Even though she was smiling in the vision, I could tell that she did not really love the man or even like him very much. She was pretending to love him for his money and status.

As I held her hand I could tell she was becoming uncomfortable. My grip was a little tighter than it should have been and the distant look on my face was not what she expected from a first meeting. I could not stop, though. I had tapped into her channel and wanted to know what made this woman tick.

In a flash her insecurities came out. I could see the poverty of her childhood, a tired and unhappy mother and a hard-working father. I could see a string of dead-end jobs that had been her life since leaving home. I could see a number of boyfriends with barely enough money to take her out on Saturday nights. This rich older man represented the end of her struggles and the beginning of life in a higher social class. Living with a man she didn't love was better than existing in a life of poverty as her mother had.

I "saw" all of this in pictures and feelings as I held this woman's hand. It was every bit as strange to me as it obviously seemed to be to her. Then I let go of her hand and made the mistake of telling her what I had seen.

Her smile wilted and her pride deflated as I described her home movie. Then a sneer came on her face as she accused me of being a private detective working for her boyfriend's children.

"Sir, who do you think you are?" she said, puffing up with dignity. "You are nothing but a Peeping Tom!"

Maybe, but how? Nothing was clear at this point in my life. I was in pain from the searing that the lightning had given me. I was also confused. The damage the lightning had done to my nervous system left me disoriented. At times I didn't know to whom I was talking, even when they were members of my immediate family. Looking back, though, I realize that those days in the hospital had a silver lining. Sometimes I jokingly refer to that time as the "good old days."

Really, though, they were the good *new* days. During this time, my life changed and I was exposed to a whole new world. While I slept, I was communicating with my spirit beings, always an adventure for me. The information they gave me and the wonders to which I was exposed as I slept was like touring an undiscovered country.

During this period, I realized I had acquired something of a sixth sense. My perceptive boundaries had been expanded. I could hear, and sometimes even see, other people's thoughts. I found it ironic that a new sense had been introduced at a time when my other senses had nearly been destroyed.

I remember the day I left the hospital. I had been in for six days and, as it turned out, had seven months of partial paralysis and therapy to look forward to. I was sitting in a wheelchair waiting for a nurse to wheel me out of the hospital to a waiting car. Wearing sunglasses to protect my eyes from the sunlight, I panted for breath because of the pain and the damage done to my heart. As I sat there, a group of people came into the room to say good-bye. They were all smiles and good wishes as they talked to me about my close call.

In my mind, though, I could hear a conversation that one of the medical staff had just had with a nurse.

"It is just as well that he go home," he said, referring to me. "The chances are slim that he is going to live much longer, anyway."

Little did he or I know at the time that I would be back.

Chapter 3

THE SIXTH SENSE

*T*hese strange events I had been experiencing intensified in a way that I did not expect once I got home. I thought everything would settle down when I returned to my own surroundings. Instead, they surprised me and did just the opposite.

As I continued to weaken physically, my mind strengthened. I still had no way to understand what was happening. It was as though I was operating outside the physical nature of the damage done to me. I still thought I was going to die, and the way I functioned as a human being was not telling me anything any different. I was sleeping about twenty hours a day and wasn't much company for those around me during the remaining four hours. I could barely walk. When I tried, I was more than likely to black out and fall down.

The days were filled with a good deal of physical pain and a lot of crawling. The emotional strain of the experience was pressing. Here I was, twenty-five, newly married, and in a single flash, I had become completely worthless.

My thoughts kept returning to where I had gone when I had died. The events tumbled through my mind, and with them came a feast of information, much of which I did not understand, and some I still do not.

With my newfound sixth sense, I was perceiving all kinds of things. When people came into the room, I experienced them differently. People appeared to me as feelings and emotions surrounded by energy; I could somehow understand them as though I were reading a book. As they talked to me there would be other forms of communications coming out of them as well. These were conversations and pictures and feelings and emotions that came from a place in their minds that only I seemed to be able to see.

Many times these events took place even when the person wasn't in the house. I think they only had to have me on their minds and I would pick up their thoughts.

About 80 percent of the time I could tell who was calling when the phone rang. I was also sometimes able to tell when people were coming to the house at least five minutes before they arrived. With many of these people, I could hear the conversations they were having as they drove to the house. I couldn't understand what was happening then. To this day, I am still trying to figure out the mechanism by which this happens.

For instance, a couple of friends were about to buy a building in a neighboring town. They wanted to get my opinion on the purchase price and the location. They decided to drop in to talk about it.

As they drove over, I could sense that they were coming. I was lying on the couch in the middle of the afternoon. I struggled to a sitting position and took a few breaths to clear my head. As I did so, I could hear their conversation.

"His family knew someone who bought the place about ten years ago," one of the men said. "I just want to know if there was anything that was wrong with the building back then."

"Who did they rent it to?" asked the other one.

"I don't know," said the first. "Maybe Dannion will remember."

By the time they got here, I knew almost everything about the building. I knew where it was and even the things that the current owner was trying to hide from them. As they came in I cut right to the chase. I told them everything about the property, including how much they should offer to pay for it.

They thanked me for the information, but I could see that they were shocked by what I knew and was able to tell them about their business. They, like everyone else, did not quite know how to adapt to the new Dannion. They were puzzled, but because they had gotten what they needed, they were pleasantly puzzled by the change.

When I was finally able to get around, going to church was an amazing experience. Even though the people were dressed in their finest clothing, the thoughts in their minds were fully exposed to me. There was something about the quiet and thoughtful nature of being in a church that laid their unconscious minds bare.

I began to visit different churches, mainly to see how the people there felt about near-death experiences.

I could sit in the back of the church and hear people thinking. When the preacher would mention something about honesty, I could hear a dozen clear thoughts from people in the pews around me about how they had done something dishonest that week.

One Sunday, while attending a church in a nearby community, I sat next to a man who owned a heating oil company. When the preacher delivered a biblical text about honesty, this man's conscience went off like a burglar alarm.

He began to think about how he was gouging the public. Although he was selling heating oil at a certain price, he was adding a few pennies to each gallon when he billed his customers. As he sat there in church, he started adding up his profits. The fact that he was cheating people and the amount he was getting in doing so frightened him. He began to wonder if this transgression would cost him in the afterlife. As he wondered, he took a few deep breaths.

How will he deal with this in his panoramic life review, I wondered.

We looked at each other when his breathing sped up. We both smiled, but there was fear in his eyes.

He tried to rationalize the theft by telling himself that he needed the extra money. That made him squirm. Finally he decided to make a large donation to the church.

*A*s I was healing, the abilities leveled off and I could pick up moods. Even if I couldn't hear what people were thinking, I could always tell how they were going to react. I knew this because I could feel the sensations that each person was feeling. For instance, I could feel one person's rising elation, while another was sliding into depression. I could feel deceit in one person and hope in another. I could feel love in one and greed in another.

I was constantly bombarded by the emotions of those people around me. No matter how people looked on the surface, I could tell how they felt inside. I did not always know why they felt that way, but I always knew how they felt.

Sometimes I didn't have enough sense to keep my mouth shut. One time a friend of my wife Sandy's came to see how I was. She was all smiles and small talk. I watched her and my wife talk excitedly in the living room. They were talking about jobs and men and having a great time doing it. Finally I had to say something, I just couldn't keep my mouth shut.

"You're unhappy about something," I said.

The two of them fell silent. My wife pursed her lips and glared at me while the other woman just stared.

"What do you mean?" she asked.

"Yeah, Dannion," said my wife. "Just *what do* you mean?"

I wished I had kept my mouth shut, but it was too late. I had to say something.

"I know you seem perfectly happy," I said. "But I am picking up the feeling that you are really unhappy about something."

It didn't take a mind reader to know that my wife was about to tell me to be quiet. Before she could speak, her friend patted her on the hand and let her true feelings show in her face.

"I haven't told anyone, but my husband and I are getting a divorce."

The two women immediately forgot what I had said and fell into a discussion of the pending divorce. I was left to ponder what had happened. Did I pick up some facial clue? Was there something in this woman's voice that betrayed her unhappiness? I just didn't know, but I continued to wonder.

I had these experiences with my wife almost every day. Being close to her had a lot to do with it, but there were other reasons I could step so easily into her world. I would usually spend the entire day sitting on the living-room couch, where I would slip into the spirit world. There I would commune with this spiritual place I had seen when my heart had stopped beating.

The spirit world must have made me sensitive to the world around me, because it was no trick to slip into Sandy's world when she came home from work. As she came into the house, I would snap out of my meditations with the spirit world and would find myself surrounded by her day. I could hear many things that she was thinking about, and see events that had happened in the last eight hours.

As she started to talk to me about her day, I would finish her sentences. Sometimes I would even begin her sentences.

One time she came home thinking of a new car. The one we had wasn't running very well, and she wanted a new one. On this day, she came home thinking of a particular car that she had never mentioned before.

When she kissed me, I could see the object of her desire, a white Ford LTD with a blue top.

"If it'll make you happy, let's get it," I said to her.

"What are you talking about?" she asked.

I described the car she was thinking about and soon we were having a discussion about how we could afford this new car.

Every time things like this happened, life between us got a little harder.

$\mathcal{I}$ was dumbfounded when these things happened. When people asked how I gained these insights, I could not answer them. Though I still don't understand these powers, I have come to accept them. The difference between the present and the way it was then is that back then they were sometimes frightening experiences.

People around me found what was happening to be unsettling. When I spoke about these strange happenings, some were very understanding. In all the times they listened to me tell about "reading other people's minds," they never became overtly upset with what I was telling them. These were real friends.

The same was true of my wife. Usually, she would listen to what I had to say, and then she would suggest that I get some professional help.

"Don't worry about it for now," she would say. Or, "If it will help you, I'll be glad to call a doctor. Maybe they can give you some medicine."

The problem was, I knew what she was thinking. It unnerved me to hear it.

This guy is going crazy was one of her thoughts.

This has got to stop was another thought that popped up all the time.

Other people thought I was crazy too. How could I blame them? I was not so sure about my sanity myself. Nothing in my life was normal. When I was asleep, I was constantly communing with the Beings of Light I had seen during my near-death experience. I could be sitting on the couch one moment and be in a spirit world the next. For example, I would find myself in a room where Spirit Beings would be working on projects. Even though I did not always understand what these Beings were doing, I could watch them as they worked. At times these spiritual voyages were like going into a classroom, at other times like going into a factory.

One time I went into a factory and watched as these Beings made structures out of light. Another time I watched as they took a single cell and grew it into a living human being. It was like watching conception, birth, and growth all in a few minutes. At other times I would find myself in a classroom where I was watching the universe in reverse, shrinking from the massive place it is to something as tiny as a pea. Other times I would go to laboratories where there appeared to be research underway that dealt with light frequencies and sound.

Where is this place? I often wondered. *What is going on? If this is the future, what a wonderful future we have.*

When I was awake, I was picking up thoughts and images from the minds of people I didn't even know.

I could look out the window of my house and pick up the thoughts of people walking down the street. Sometimes I would go to the supermarket with someone. I would sit in the car and listen to the radio while my friend shopped. I could hear the thoughts of people as they walked back to their cars.

I was amazed by how negatively people viewed themselves. I still am. Beginning in those early days, it became clear to me that most people have a very low opinion of themselves. As I watched people go in and out of the store, I could hear their self-impressions. Most of their feelings were negative. They all seemed to feel guilty about something or another that they had done in their lives. Many felt they had done wrong things in their lives or that life had beaten them down so much that they felt inferior. I could tell that they never allowed themselves to touch themselves spiritually. Instead, they focused on the surface things in their lives and picked themselves apart. Person after person, I could hear them think that they were ugly, overweight, or poor, or bad parents, or just downright dumb. *I sure hope shopping doesn't do that to everyone,* I thought.

Rarely did the people whose thoughts I was picking up focus on what great and powerful spiritual beings they were. Few took credit for their greatness. I began to realize that people have almost a need to feel guilty, wrong, or inferior, and that this need seems to overwhelm any consideration that they are spiritual beings. Instead, they see themselves as being trapped in a reality that is controlled and manipulated by everybody else. I often wondered how much the system had to do with their low self-opinions—institutions from government to religion are always expressing people's inadequacy. And amazingly, people seem to accept that judgment.

This sense of being controlled caused a lot of stress in people. Even those who accepted it still held a grudge. They felt unimportant, as though they were just cogs in the machine of society.

I found that the more stress a person was under, the more perceptive I was. I still am. This is especially true of people dealing with grief or trauma, but any kind of stress functions as a transmitter. I don't know what causes this, I just know that it comes to me that way. Maybe it is just that stress has a way of opening a person up to being "read."

One night I went to one of my nephew's ball games just to get out of the house. I was barely able to move in those days, but attending his Little League ball games was a big event for me.

As I sat there, a boy walked past me. I looked at him and could feel fear and loathing as he walked to the other end of the stands and sat down. I was surprised to be picking up his feelings so strongly, since I usually did not read kids. I focused on him for a moment. I could tell that he was afraid of somebody who was wearing a yellow jacket. There were other people in his mind, too, but his main fear was of this boy in the jacket. Something had transpired between these two, and now the boy in the jacket was coming with his friends to beat up this boy.

I looked around and couldn't see anyone in a yellow jacket. *Am I going nuts?* I thought. *Am I seeing something that doesn't exist?*

I craned my neck around and saw three boys come around the corner of the stands. Then out came a fourth. He was wearing the yellow jacket. I motioned him over.

"Are you looking for that guy?" I asked, pointing to the kid at the end of the stands.

"Yeah," said the kid in the yellow jacket.

"You gonna beat him up?" I asked.

"Yeah," said the kid. He had a puzzled grin on his face. He was stunned by the question and by who had asked it. For one thing, he didn't know who I was. For another, he had never before seen someone as feeble as I was.

"Well, leave him alone," I said. "I know there are security cops here tonight."

These experiences were deeply confusing. Here I was, struggling to get well. I was so badly damaged that I could do little more than sleep and eat. I had to relearn everything. I not only had to figure out how to walk, but I had to figure out what world it was that I was going to walk in. Some days I would make it out to the couch and write in a notebook all day. I was driven to do this.

Thoughts were coming fast and furious, and I had to get them down on paper before I forgot them.

I soon realized that I was in three worlds: the spirit world, my own world, and the world of whoever was around me.

As I healed and began to get around, I came to accept these experiences as a normal part of my being. Some of the people around me also began to accept the changes in me.

If I started telling a stranger what he was thinking, many times it was just an attempt to tell if what I was seeing was real. My friends would usually step in and say that I had been "slightly altered" by the lightning strike.

"Well if he is so 'altered,' then how does he know what I am thinking about?" demanded one stranger.

I finally came to accept it. I had some form of extra perception.

Chapter 4

MY THREE WORLDS

Sometimes I would just sit and cry. I was so overwhelmed by it all and didn't understand what had happened to me. I had physical problems, yet I had acquired perceptive abilities that increased my reach far beyond what it had ever been. The lightning had scrambled my thought processes so much that sometimes I was unable to carry on a conversation with a person who was in the room. Yet my communications with the Spirit Beings I had seen after I was struck by lightning were always clear and concise.

I was living in three worlds, and none of them felt like home. This went on for more than ten months. Only then did I hear of the near-death experience and could begin to put what was going on into some context.

Until that understanding, my life was positively bizarre.

In my real world, I had become a child all over again. I still slept all day. "The sleep of the dead," my friends called it, because I did not budge. I did not dream at all. Either the lightning had burned the capacity to dream right out of me or my body was so tired from healing that it didn't have the energy for this extracurricular activity.

I walked with great effort. I had to use a cane to get out of bed, and needed to balance myself against the walls to make it down the hall. I had to think about every step I took. If I didn't, I ran the risk of falling. One day, for instance, I inched down the hall and started thinking about what I was going to have for breakfast instead of where my feet were going. The next thing I knew I was flat on my face in the hallway. It seemed as though everything that used to be automatic now required my full attention.

Most of my days were spent on the living-room sofa. That was the easiest place to be, since I was usually tired by the time I got out of bed and down the hall.

I knew I was in the real world when I sat on the couch. I could feel the couch against my back and smell the smells in the room. These were simple smells like furniture polish or fresh flowers. They helped ground me in the real world.

There were other things as well that kept me grounded. I would put objects on the table and touch them periodically. These were simple things: a tiny pyramid, a pincushion, a Bible, a calculator. Also I used bottles of fragrance to help orient my sense of smell, a form of what is known as aromatherapy. I developed ways to assure myself that I was in this world.

The spirit world was **very** different.

I experienced it first in tones, like music played on an organ. Then I would start to focus on something like the window, or one of the objects on the table. At first I consciously focused on the object. Then I had the feeling of leaving the physical world. In every way it was like the straps of a straitjacket coming off and my body being freed from bondage. I left the confines of my physical body and felt totally unrestrained and free.

I would feel the Spirit Beings. I could see them whether I had my eyes open or closed, although I could see them better with my eyes open. They did not talk to me. Instead, they unfolded the information in front of me in a way that made me feel as if I was a part of the information, yet was detached at the same time. To this day I don't know what 90 percent of the information meant, even though I dutifully wrote down as much of it as I could.

I would see things throughout the day. It was as though I was passing through a great library where I became the pages in a book. There would be equations that I didn't understand and information that was impossible for me to comprehend. Even now, when I look back at those notes from that period I wonder what was going on.

The one comfort I had in those days was panoramic life review. That was the one thing from the real world that I could cling to. When things got bad, when I didn't know whether I was coming or going, I could always look back over the experience of dying and find solace in everything that had happened, from being out of my body to having the life review.

At first I wasn't sure why I found such comfort in the life review. Then it became clear to me: The life review was the only thing I had taken with me. It was the only thing that was from this side that went with me through the tunnel both times when I died.

I had seen my life pass before me and could now gain a perspective on it from the values I had been exposed to on the other side.

The ability to review my life and infuse it with the spiritual values I had learned on the other side is what made me a whole person. In essence, the panoramic life review gave me the opportunity to examine things in my life that had bothered me and put them into a spiritual context. The process can do the same for you.

With each review, I could feel my own self-centeredness and the pain I had caused others. I became aware of the spiritual awakening to which my life reviews led.

I came to understand that we were all a part of a central fabric. We have individual purpose, but we have a group purpose as well. By looking back on my life, I could see how interactions set patterns by which things would unfold later. Reflecting back on my life was almost like watching the ripple effect in reverse.

I also learned the power of empathy, and saw it as one of the most important lessons that can be learned through life review. Empathy is a person's ability to sympathize with another's feelings and attitudes. Through life review, I gained this ability to see another person's point of view and feel the way they felt. That allowed me to be free of guilt and other emotions when dealing with people, to look at others from a sort of middle ground.

I could not get a grip on what was going on. I didn't know how to interpret what was going on or how to control it. Had I gone crazy? Was I possessed? Was this a natural part of me? Could this happen to everybody?

Now I realize that this was a gift from the spirit world. To this day I live in three worlds and have learned to enjoy it tremendously. Through all the pain and confusion, I know that there is a spiritual life and that we are all an integral part of that life. I learned that there is a world after this one, and that it lives over here, too, through us. Our connection to that world is the breath we breathe. Such a simple thing as breath allows us to be connected to the other side, no matter which side we are on. I also learned that I was able to perceive things about people and about what was going on in their lives.

I am always trying to control certain aspects of living in these three worlds and not let the things I can't control drive me crazy. The only place I have found where these three worlds connect is in a hospice, which is where I spend time with people who are dying. It is there that people nearing the ends of their lives make a connection with the spirit world. By being with dying people, I am able to share in their world as they pass over to the other side. As they transfer to their spiritual side, they are actually living in two worlds at the same time. A person who does hospice work lives in those worlds with the dying.

It is in hospice work that a person can realize that death is not to be feared.

In the early days, I had no understanding about what was happening. I knew only that I had no control over the things that were coming into my mind.

In looking back I realize that my experience was like flying an airplane without first being given lessons. I was bound to crash, and crash I did.

Until I finally earned my wings, I crashed hard.

Chapter 5

THE CRASH

I did not have a sense of the uses of these powers of perception. I was interested in exploring the reach of my sixth sense, but it never crossed my mind that there was a negative side to having these abilities. I didn't know that by applying the powers in a certain way I could affect other people in either a positive or a negative sense. Instead, I was just interested in learning about and using the powers.

I could use my ability to read the thoughts of others in ways that helped my friends. In a number of instances, I could listen to people during business negotiations and tell if they were actually going to deliver on the promises they had made.

One time, a friend planned to buy a number of water purifiers for resale. I happened to be with him when he went to complete the deal. The man who was selling the purifiers promised two-week delivery and an additional 20 percent discount if my friend paid him on the spot. I tried to get my friend's attention as he wrote out the check, but he ignored me and gave the man the check.

"That guy's a crook," I said to my friend.

"No way," he said. "You just don't believe anyone."

I told him that the salesman needed money and that he was making promises he couldn't keep to everyone who came along just to pick their pockets. I also told him that the salesman had no guilt about stealing this money from people.

"He thinks the world owes him a living," I said. "That's exactly what he was thinking."

"Want to bet?" my friend asked. I put a hundred dollars on what I heard the man thinking while my friend bet on what he had said. About three weeks later, the friend grudgingly gave me the hundred dollars. "You were right," he said sheepishly. "The check was cashed, and now his telephone has been disconnected. He robbed me."

After that it wasn't uncommon for friends to drop in and ask me questions about business or personal finance. Should I buy this car? Does it make sense to buy this building? Am I going to get ripped off by this or that salesman? I became an underground business adviser. People who asked me about their business matters rarely admitted it to other people. I didn't care. I knew that they didn't want to admit that they were relying on something other than a business plan or a well-thought-out family budget to decide on how to spend their money.

The Crash

I didn't mind, I was trying to help. At first I didn't understand my abilities. Using them to make business decisions gave me an opportunity to put them to the test. In a very short period of time, I could tell whether my advice was good or not. I was pleased to note that, with all things considered, I made few mistakes in the business arena.

Making these kinds of decisions helped me gain confidence in my powers. As my understanding grew, so did the confidence in my abilities. I began to predict the outcome of all kinds of events with great accuracy. I remember predicting the winners of a number of afternoon baseball games over the course of one week and having almost all of them be correct.

On one occasion, I was watching televised bowling with a friend. As the bowler made his run up to the line, I muttered the outcome of the roll. "Seven pins," I would say, or "Strike," or "Gutter ball." I was right at least 95 percent of the time.

"That's pretty amazing," said the friend. "We should do that for money."

Soon word of my abilities got around. My popularity grew. Suddenly people wanted to be around me, especially when there was a sporting event to bet on. They invited me to bars to watch football and baseball games, even to bowling alleys on league nights. There were few of my friends who did not want to show up when I decided to go to the horse races.

They loved having me around so they could win and, frankly, I loved being around them. It was now years after the lightning strike and I was ready to get out. I was still relying on a cane for the support my legs couldn't give me and sunglasses because my eyes were hypersensitive to sunlight. Still, I had to get out. I was tired of living like a hermit.

Using my abilities to gamble made me one of the boys again. I was able to get out of the house and resume a normal pattern of thoughts. Instead of spending the day sitting on a couch talking to Spirit Beings, I was now able to go out and talk about the sorts of things that guys talk about.

My gambling prowess brought me a lot of friends. People came to talk to me about upcoming sporting events. Some would bring racing forms and football schedules and talk about the games. Others just wanted to talk about their favorite teams.

I liked it best when they offered to take me out of the house. Sometimes they took me to a bar or restaurant where we watched a game. Sometimes I was taken to the sporting event itself. Even though I was a physical burden, I was always treated very well.

Sometimes, though, friends just got me out of the house so I could enjoy myself. One of these trips was to Jacksonville, Florida, with three friends who took me along so I could have a change of scene.

The Crash

This was an act of pure friendship. I was in no shape for a trip like this one and was a definite handicap to their enjoyment. I weighed about 160 pounds and was still subject to blackouts. I could be sitting there talking one minute and then fall flat on my face in the next instant. I could easily have blacked out at the dog track in Florida and died right there in the midst of a quinella. So for these guys to take me on such a trip meant that they really cared about me.

I decided to do them a favor.

I asked them to give me a racing form. As they sat and waited, I marked up the form, showing the dogs that would win. Somehow, by looking at a list of the dogs and then at the dogs themselves, I could tell which ones were going to win. I didn't understand why I could do that, and I still don't understand. I only know that it happens.

By the end of the day, we had won more than $3,000. Everyone was happy, myself included. I had been able to give something back to some true friends.

I did remain puzzled by how I was consistently able to pick winners. Eventually, I came to understand some aspects of my abilities. For instance, I realized that if the event involved living beings, I could predict the outcome. If an event had dogs, horses, people—anything with life—then my odds of knowing the outcome were twice as good as just picking numbers. I cannot predict the spin of a roulette wheel, for instance, but stand me in front of a row of blackjack dealers and I can usually tell what the facedown card is. I have to have a human or some other living being with which to communicate. The more emotional the being, the better.

Clearly, I communicate with people, not machines. Elements like will and skill are somehow communicated in whatever I pick up.

I made a true believer of a small-time hustler. One afternoon we were watching a pro football game in which his team was ahead twenty-one to nothing in the third quarter. The hustler was elated. His money riding on the team that was winning, he thought he was going to win a mountain of cash.

I could sense that his optimism was premature. Something came through the screen to me that told me the game was going to turn around. I could see the score, and the fact that his team was going to lose by one point. Call it spirit, or skill, or just a glimpse of the future, I don't know what it was, but in my mind I could sense a change in the other team. I knew this was going to be a bad day for the hustler.

"This game is going to turn around," I said to him.

He looked at me with anger. "Don't say that," he said. "Talk like that makes it happen."

"It's already happened," I said. "Your boys are out of gas."

Slowly but surely it became obvious that I was right. Four touchdowns later, the hustler's team left the field defeated and he told me that I had to leave.

"You're nothing but bad luck, Dannion," he said, showing me the door. "If it wasn't for you, they would have won."

It had nothing to do with me. I was only the messenger of future events. Somehow I had picked up the dedication, focus, and intensity of both teams. Somewhere in my mind, these factors combined to let me know who the victors would be. I was amazed by what was going on, but I realized that it was simply a by-product of what was happening in the spiritual side. My new powers came from a change in focus and direction.

This sudden ability to gamble was a surprise to me.

I had never been a gambler. I didn't play cards, or the horses. I really had no interest in betting on football games. To tell the truth, I didn't even like to watch football games. Even now, it is a rare day when I can sit down and watch any kind of ball game for more than twenty or thirty minutes.

Suddenly, though, I had an edge that I had to use. I wondered why I was given this ability. Was there a way that I could use it to raise my consciousness? I began to solicit the opinion of many friends, and I got a wide variety of answers.

"Use it to win a lot of money," said one friend.

"Then you can live free and have money," said another friend.

Yet another friend offered a suggestion that spread the money out a little. "You can make a lot of money for yourself, that's obvious," he said. "But every time you make money for yourself, make it for other people too. When you place a bet for yourself, place one for a poor person. That way, you can elevate them too."

The most commonly suggested use of my powers was this: "Help me make a lot of money, and I in turn will donate half of it to a charity."

I did that a number of times and never once saw it work. When I used my powers to help people make money, they never lived up to their end of the bargain. Instead they would spend it all on themselves and come back with an excuse as to why they didn't do what they had promised.

I'll give you a couple of examples.

I was approached once by a teacher and a doctor from another town. They had heard about me and wanted to know if they could tap my resources to win some bets they had on a number of college football games.

"I'll do it on one condition," I said. "If you win more than a thousand dollars, you have to promise to give half of your winnings to a men's shelter."

They quickly agreed. I sat down with them and looked at the game sheet that the teacher had written out. About an hour later they left to place their bets with a local hustler.

In all, they won over $5,000. Two weeks later they came back for more.

"Did you give the men's shelter half the money?" I asked.

To their credit, they told the truth. "No, we didn't," said the teacher. "But we promise that next time we'll give almost all of the money to the shelter."

I decided not to help them again, which left both of them feeling hurt.

"Once a fool, twice an idiot," I told them. "If you didn't donate the money the first time, you surely won't do it the second time."

*W*ith another gambler I tried a more direct approach. He had taken me to a restaurant on a Sunday to watch the professional football games. He was hot to gamble and even hotter to win. He hadn't won a meaningful bet in a long time and thought that he was due.

He began to push me for the winner of the day's best game. At first I was silent. Then I hit on an idea.

"I'll tell you who to bet on if you give half of your winnings to that bum who hangs out in front of the post office," I said.

The gambler thought a minute and then nodded. "Why not?" he said. "Sounds fair, anyway."

I told him who to bet on and then we watched with anxiety as a tight game came down in his favor.

He was delighted at his victory and bought

drinks for everyone at the table. Before the drinks came, I left the table to go to the men's room. As I came back, I saw him going out the door and turning away from the post office.

"He had to get home," one of the guys at the table said. "But he said to say thanks."

With all the people I helped to win money, few ever gave any of their money to charity. If they had any kind of reason for not keeping their promise, it was always a lame one. They needed the money more than the charity did. Or they had heard that the charity they were considering mismanaged money. Or, "That bum will just spend it all on booze."

I wish I could say that I couldn't understand how these people felt, but I could. In fact, I couldn't point an accusing finger at them without pointing one at myself. I, like all the others, was spending my gambling winnings on myself. I used the same excuses to keep the money for myself. I even threw in one that they couldn't use: Because I had been struck by lightning, I deserved the extra money that the Beings of Light were now giving me.

*D*espite my rationalizations, I began to feel very empty in the gambling world. It had never been my world, and I now realized that it could never be my world. Part of it was my parents. They were always against gambling. They felt, and rightfully so, that your odds of winning were slim.

Even though the odds were now in my favor, their words continued to play in my ear. "Gambling is a waste of your talent. But worse, it's a waste of your time. Spend your life doing real work."

Also, I didn't have the patience to be a gambler. I had to spend too much time looking at racing forms or thinking about the spread for different games. Frankly, it didn't interest me that much. Even though I was making money, it truly did seem like a waste of time.

Even worse were the people who were obsessed with gambling. At first I enjoyed just getting out of the house. I didn't care who I was with. After a while, I realized that gamblers live in a very cynical and snide world. Perhaps I belonged in that world at one time, but things had changed for me now. My near-death experience had transformed me in ways that I did not understand. I knew that I didn't belong with gamblers, but at the same time I didn't know exactly where I did belong.

For seven months, I gambled avidly and made money doing it. I bought a new car and a number of other things that we could not afford before I started playing the odds.

It was not uncommon for me to come home from one of these gambling forays and have money to pay the bills. As you can well imagine, this made me extremely happy. I felt as if I were finally making a comeback. We had gone a year now without my being able to work. Even though the doctors' bills continued to mount, I was beginning to feel like the breadwinner again.

I tried hard to rationalize the gambling to myself. So what if the money was from gambling? So what if I was using these strange powers to get back on my feet? I deserved to have a little fun and profit after nearly dying. Let the good times roll. It was my turn to make money, and it did not matter how I did it.

Those were the excuses I gave for gambling.

In reality, I was starting to hate the way I was being used by others to gamble. In my spiritual self, I knew that there was no excuse for what I was doing.

Chapter 6

A Clear Mission

Although my exact mission was clear to me, my understanding of it was not. I knew that making money through my perceptive insights was not what I was supposed to be doing with my special powers.

The event that hammered that point home was a simple one. I went to the dog track with a group of my friends. With them was a fellow I didn't know very well named Charles. He had heard that I could pick winners at the track, and he wanted some of the action. As we sat there watching the races, he got pushy. He wanted me to pick a winner for him and he got incredibly demanding about it. Nowadays when that happens I tell people to forget it. Back then, I was still looking for someone who was honest. I told him I would help him under my usual condition.

"You have to take half the winnings and donate them to charity," I said. Not surprisingly, he agreed.

By the end of the day he had won several thousand dollars.

I wished I had never helped this guy. After collecting his money at the redemption window, he began to cackle like a rooster as he waved the bills around and showed them to the other people in line.

He was insufferable to be with on the way home. All he could talk about was what a great job of handicapping he had done and how wrong members of his family were to say that he had a gambling problem. "It's no problem if you're winning like this," he insisted.

I was glad when we finally dropped him off. His wife probably felt differently, though. Someone told me later that he went into the house and threw the money down on the table in front of her. Then he started in on the poor woman. He insisted that this money proved that his gambling was not a bad habit. He derided her for being critical of him and said that maybe she needed more courage instead of his needing psychological help with his gambling. He had used this hollow victory to rationalize everything his gambling had taken away from his family. Now, instead of going back and giving the money to them with love, he was gloating.

When I heard from others what he had said, I was sickened. Not only did he not donate any of his winnings to charity, but he was now insisting that I had not helped him at all.

"We put both of our heads together to win that money," was the most credit he would give me. Other than that, he denied that I had contributed to his winnings.

This sickening experience was the last straw for me. I had known all along that most of my new friends were showing an interest in me because I could improve their financial situations. I didn't care. It was nice to have people around, no matter what their motives.

With this incident, I realized how tired I had become of my new friends who were interested in my gift only for what it could give them. I realized that no matter how much fun we were having, what was really on their minds was the simple question: How can we use him without looking at where this ability comes from?

I had been put off by this attitude from the very beginning, but I had tolerated it. Now it had become tiresome, and I felt shallow. I realized that I was in the midst of a spiritual crisis and could no longer deal with people who liked me only for how they could use me.

After this realization, I turned my back on these uses of my abilities and walked away. When "friends" called, I told them I was busy. If they challenged me and said I had lost the special abilities, I shrugged and let them believe what they wanted. I didn't want them around anyway. Redefining my mission was now my goal. I knew it would be difficult, but I vowed to let the search continue.

And continue it did.

My intuitive abilities were not the only thing that my near-death experience had left me with to figure out. I had been given a tremendous amount of information by the Spirit Beings during my near-death experience and the period of my recuperation.

Some of the information was incomprehensible. To this day I cannot figure out the meaning of the extensive notes I took in those first months. I liken much of what went on to *Math Magicland,* a Walt Disney feature in which Donald Duck is bombarded by mathematical equations. On a daily basis, I felt like Donald Duck in that movie, as numbers rained down from the heavens and appeared in visions. The difference was that it was not a cartoon, and I couldn't stop it.

Some of my notebook pages are just long lists of numbers that make no sense to me at all. Others are filled with information that relates to the creation of "Centers," where people could come to reduce the stress in their lives. By doing this, the thirteenth Being of Light told me, we could realize that we are powerful spiritual beings.

The Spirit Being told me that the creation of these Centers was to be my mission on earth. "You are to engage in this coming system by changing people's thought processes," he said. "Show people how to rely on their spiritual selves. Religion is fine, but don't let yourself be entirely controlled by it. Humans are mighty spiritual beings. All they need to realize is that love is the most powerful force."

I had a vision of the rooms that these Centers were to consist of. It was a puzzling vision, to be sure.

One of the rooms was a therapy room in which people would gather and talk to each other. Humor was definitely invited into this room, since the purpose here was to break the ice and relax about the search for our spiritual sides. Without humor, the search for spirituality can be a long and painful affair.

Another room was devoted to massage. In here, people would be massaged as well as massage others. The purpose of this, said the Spirit Beings, was to illustrate that we could cross the physical boundaries of strangers and provide pleasure instead of the discomfort that most people feel when they are touched by someone they don't know.

A sensory deprivation system made up another room. This soothing environment would allow people to go deep within themselves and examine physical and mental feelings they were not ordinarily in touch with.

I will say now that I am amazed by the deep emotions that emerge through sensory deprivation. Good sensory deprivation allows a person's senses to be completely without sensory input. The person's weight is supported in great comfort, and there is no sound or other stimuli.

When there is no sensory input, there is a great deal of psychological output. The lack of physical stimulation allows the spiritual and the human mind to release things that are troubling. I have seen people recover forgotten memories of long-ago events, which then helped them to progress and become the sort of people they wanted to become.

Biofeedback equipment made up another room. Through this equipment, people would learn that they could control their emotions as well as the ways in which their bodies reacted to these emotions.

Another room matched patients with people who had intuitive powers and who could provide personal insights. Once these insights were out in the open, patients would be open for further discussion of deep feelings and emotions. They could touch their emotional, spiritual, and physical sides all at the same time.

A bed made of seven components made up the next room. With this bed, a person could relax so deeply that he could actually leave his body. This was the most puzzling of all the devices. Although I could see it clearly, it took years for the Spirit Beings to reveal all of the components to me. I had many struggles after being struck by lightning, but none took so long and perplexed me so much as this one. I searched for years for ways in which to perfect this bed, and I am still not sure it is as good as it should be.

I have now completed a third version of the bed and continue to be astonished by its results. I'll deal with those results later in the book. I will say now, however, that every modification I make opens the door to better results. And many of the improvements I make are guided by the Spirit Beings.

Another room remains a puzzle to me, as well. It was a reflection chamber made of polished steel or copper shaped in such a way that the person inside could not see his own reflection. To this day, I do not entirely understand the purpose of this room.

The Spirit Being claimed that the purpose of these rooms was "to show people that they can be in control of their lives through God."

The vision I had on the other side firmly imprinted an image of each of these rooms in my mind. Yet for all the crystal clarity that this vision had, no blueprint for The Centers was given to me. Instead, the Being told me that the components for these rooms would come to me over the years. When I saw them, I would recognize their purpose and put them in their proper place. Eventually I would have all of the components necessary to carry out my mission.

"Eventually" has turned out to be twenty years. In the course of that time I have found myself looking for things of an unknown nature. Every time something caught my eye I thought of it in terms of The Centers. This often made me crazy. Does it belong somewhere in those rooms? I would ask myself. Am I interested in this object because it belongs in the vision?

Finding the unknown components of The

Centers became an obsession with me. It was my stated mission. If I were to believe that I had been in a heavenly place and in the presence of Beings of Light when I died, then I had to do what they told me to do.

*S*ome simple truths about life and the event that nearly took it became clear at this point. With this added clarity came new values for myself. This change was accomplished because of my life review during my near-death experience. When that happened, I was able to examine my life from a third-person perspective. I could see how I had affected others and how they had affected me. I could see the good I had done as well as the bad. I could see myself as each person I had encountered and feel the direct results of my action. I could tell the right actions from the wrong.

The life review allowed me to examine my life without having my ego involved. This lack of ego involvement, and the increased empathy, enabled me to make a totally honest appraisal of all the aspects of my life.

In some ways the effects of this review were similar to psychotherapy. Instead of taking several years, though, it took only seconds or perhaps minutes. Still, it was an extremely effective form of transformation. By examining my life from a distance, I was able to make significant changes in who I was and what I valued.

A Clear Mission

I knew I had to disseminate this information about the life review to others. Somehow this was part of my mission.

$\mathcal{M}$y brush with the gambling world gave me a very powerful clue as to what another part of my mission was to be. Even though I detested gambling, I realized that it is as close as many people get to their spiritual side. I have seen that clearly over the years. When I visit Las Vegas now for speaking engagements, I am amazed by the feelings I get from people as I walk through the casinos. The atmosphere is charged with feelings of hope and chance, luck and potential.

I realized back then, as I know now, that if I could get people as excited about spiritual matters as they are about winning a few coins at slot machines or the dog track, then I could make positive changes in the world.

I knew that I had been brought back for a purpose, and that the creation of The Centers was only part of that mission. The question I was left with was the same that so many people have: Why am I here? I finally began in earnest to follow the trail of clues that the Spirit Beings had given me.

And as I followed the trail, I found the meaning of life.

Chapter 7

THE BRIGHT SIDE
OF MYSTERY

*M*y intuitive powers could not be turned "on" or "off" at will. This made for some confusing moments. Sometimes I read the wrong person in a crowd. Sometimes I would perceive things and misinterpret them. Sometimes I thought I would go crazy from the sensory overload. Being in a crowded room, for instance, was sometimes more than I could take. It was like being surrounded by twenty televisions and trying to watch all of them at the same time.

When I found myself trying to pay attention to everything I was picking up, I felt as if I were going insane. These were the days before I learned how to cope with this sensory overload and it was not easy. *If I can perceive it, why can't I interpret it?* I wondered.

Sometimes I would try to drink these powers away. I realize now that this was a form of self-medication that often worked. At times I found myself too drunk to function as a human being, let alone a human being with extrasensory perceptions.

Sometimes, drinking didn't help. Even drunk, I would have previews of future events.

One night I was in a Washington, D.C., bar talking to a couple of businessmen. After several drinks, I had begun to relax. As I listened to these two men talk, a vision began to appear in my mind.

I saw a car, a 1976 Camaro, speeding down a rain-soaked road. Suddenly the car ahead of it began to cross a bridge and just disappeared! Then the Camaro drove right off, just behind the other car and into the water.

It was just a brief image, like a snippet of film from a television program. Yet it was so vivid that I couldn't get it out of my mind. Since I had picked it up while listening to these two fellows talk, I just butted in on their conversation.

"Excuse me. Do either one of you drive a 1976 Camaro?" I asked.

"I do," said one of the men.

"And how are you going to go home?" I asked.

By now they had stopped their conversation and were giving me the evil eye. As one of the two men described his route home, I interrupted again.

"Is there a bridge on the way that has wooden planks running across it?"

"Draw it," he said.

I took out a pen and drew an odd little bridge on a napkin. It was a crude rendering, but there were features that one of the men recognized.

"Yeah," he said. "There is a place near my house that looks just like that."

I didn't quite know what to do. I fumbled around for a few seconds and then decided, *What the hell.* I told them what I had seen. It made me uncomfortable. I did not want to have these perceptions, just as I did not now want to tell these guys what I had seen. In a way, the visions made me feel responsible for whatever happened to them. One thing I didn't want was that responsibility, especially at a life and death level.

"Tell us that story again," said one of the men.

I told them what I had seen. I must have been filled with emotion as I told them because they drew back and looked at me with a sort of fear on their faces.

"Why don't you stay with me, guys," I offered. "You've had too much to drink to drive safely, anyway. Just stay at my place tonight."

They agreed to do that and stayed until morning. The next day, one of them called me from his home in Virginia. A bridge on his route home had rusted through and fallen apart. That night two cars had driven off the bridge and three people had been injured.

Why I had seen their car drive off the bridge I don't know. I do believe that I somehow altered the future by having this vision. And I know two fellows who are glad to have been with me that night.

Things like this happened again and again. I heard that a friend was going to rent an airplane with a turbo-charged engine just to see how it performed.

I didn't think much about this when I first heard it. Later in the day, however, the friend called me again to talk about something else. As he did, a vision came into my mind. I could see an engine running that had a wide belt with grooves on it. In a few moments, the belt broke and jammed the engine. There was a grinding sound and a pop as the engine stopped.

Does this mean his plane is going to crash? I wondered this as I spoke to him on the telephone. Rather than say nothing at all, I decided to risk looking foolish and tell him what I had seen in my mind.

He decided not to rent the airplane. Later that day, someone else did. As they started the engine and revved it for takeoff, the belt broke loose and the engine caught on fire. Fortunately, no one was hurt.

*I*n the early days it was difficult to act on these premonitions, mainly because I didn't know how to approach people about the visions I had had. Sometimes I wish I had been more forceful in telling potential victims of the future, just what it was I had seen or perceived.

One time in my dad's store I saw a woman walking down one of the aisles. Riding in her grocery cart was a child with curly blond hair wearing a polka-dotted outfit.

As I looked at her, a vision began to form in my mind. I saw this child and her mother riding down the street in a white Volvo station wagon. Suddenly I saw the little girl fall out of the passenger door and hit the pavement hard.

I saw this horrifying scene in a split second and didn't know what to make of it. The only thing I knew to do was to approach the woman.

"Excuse me," I said to her. "Do you drive a white Volvo station wagon?"

I must have been fairly nervous when I asked the question because she seemed unnerved by my sudden presence. Did she think I was a stalker? Or a salesman? I'll never know. She pushed her child out of the store and toward a white Volvo.

About half a mile down the road, the woman's station wagon was hit broadside by a pickup truck. The woman was injured. The child was thrown from the car, but was not badly hurt.

There were other visions that I didn't act upon. Indeed, even ones that I could not act upon.

One time I was coming off the interstate in Atlanta when in my mind I saw two cars collide and a woman get thrown out of one of the cars.

I was apprehensive because I knew that I would see that very accident any minute now. *But why, why is this happening?* I wondered. As the exit road curved and went over the freeway, there ahead was the very accident I had already seen.

I got to the woman and helped her the best I could. As I administered first aid, though, I was baffled by the fact that I had already seen the accident in my head. *Was I still in my head now?* I wondered. Was I actually giving first aid or was this event just playing out in my mind?

I was often confused about what was really happening and what was, well, an event from the future.

One day I was crossing the street in Charleston, South Carolina, when an event played out vividly in my head. I saw a man crossing the same street I was crossing, and behind him I saw two girls about to step off the curb and follow him. Suddenly a big yellow Chrysler came swerving down the road and hit the two girls. One of them was carried along on the hood and then crushed between the Chrysler and a parked car.

I could tell in the vision that the car was being driven by an old woman who had simply lost control of her car as she was making a turn.

I was almost to the other side of the street when this vision appeared in my mind. It was just like a memory of something that had already happened, a memory of something I had witnessed. I stopped and turned around.

Suddenly I realized that the vision was about to happen in real life. Behind me were the two girls I had seen in my mind. Down the street came the ancient yellow Chrysler. I then realized that the man I had seen in my mind was me! I was living the vision.

"Hey! Stop!" I shouted to the girls. I ran at them with my hands up. They were shocked to see me approaching them with my hands up. They backed up, and as they did, the yellow Chrysler crossed between us and slammed into the parked car just around the corner.

Events like these posed very serious philosophical questions for me. Visions like this one showed that in one way or another, the future had already happened. The puzzling thing to me, however, was that I seemed to be able to change the future by acting on the visions that I saw. What exactly did this mean? Was it wrong to change the future, or was I meant to do it for reasons that I didn't understand?

*S*ometimes the results of reporting on these visions were quite humorous. If these visions are really a gift from the spirit world, then they are proof that those on the other side have a great sense of humor.

Two women came to see me one time about a problem one of them was having with her husband.

"I think my husband is having an affair," one of them said as the other stood behind her and nodded.

I shrugged and took the woman's hand. "Let me see what I see," I said. I took the woman's hand and looked off into the distance. The image of a house came into my mind. I described it to the woman who was sitting before me. *Why am I picking up information about this woman's husband through her?* I wondered. I continued.

I described the way it looked outside and then went into the front door.

"This house that I am looking at is odd," I said. "It has blue furniture and brown carpeting. This is really an ugly house."

The woman who was standing became nervous, and the one sitting became agitated.

"You're having an affair with my husband!" she shouted at her friend. A heated argument ensued. By the time I got them out of the house, I realized that these powers had the ability to destroy friendships as well as build them up, and to save people as well as let them go down the drain.

For the most part, the perceptions I had, and still have, are not full of drama. What I see is ordinary stuff. I see how people go through their days, or things that are meaningful in their lives, like their relationships with their children or the way they truly feel about their husbands. Now I am able to ignore most of this information and not comment on it. By not commenting on everything I see, I am then not obligated to be a part of it.

In the early days I was not smart enough to keep my mouth shut. When I sat in a restaurant and could perceive that a waitress had had a fight with her boyfriend that morning, I felt some kind of inner duty to say something about it. As a result, I found myself counseling people constantly.

In essence I was "on" all the time and felt a need always to talk about my perceptions. Of course, I was also pushed a great deal to be on. When I was around other people, they often wanted to know how they could use my powers to make money or to make some kind of personal decisions.

Such demands put a good deal of pressure on me, which continues to this day. I had to get an unlisted telephone number, for instance, because I received as many as a hundred calls a day from people who wanted to know what their futures held or simply wanted to know the right thing to do. I wish I could have helped them all.

Most people don't really need help, from a psychic or a psychologist, in solving their problems. More often than not I tell people to try and figure out their own problems. I remind them of what the Beings of Light told me about humans, that we are all great and powerful spiritual beings who sometimes forget our own spiritual strengths.

"Put all of the mundane things in your life aside," I will commonly tell someone who thinks he or she needs my perceptive abilities. "For just a few minutes put aside all of the petty things that go on in your job, ignore the way your kids are acting, put all of your baggage with your spouse on hold, and try to look at your spirit, or think of something you love. If you try to please your spirit, which is your real self, then most decisions are not that tough to make. You can sometimes see the possible future when you do that. It is when you try to please everyone in your life instead of your spiritual self that you end up in spiritual crisis."

Sometimes I still feel a responsibility to speak up. And sometimes it gets me into deep trouble.

One morning, for instance, I was filling a car with gas at the gas station when a woman pulled up in a car next to me. She smiled at me and said hello, but I could tell that she was extremely upset.

"Having a good day, so far?" I asked.

"I've had better," she said. "But this one will do."

Quite literally, we began to talk about the weather. As she spoke, I matched the tone of her voice to a tone that I produce in my own throat. To those around me, this sounds like a faint hum. For me, it is the way I make a perceptive connection with someone through their speech. I don't know how it works or why, but it is almost as effective as touching them.

As I matched her tone I could see the things in her life that were bothering her. Her husband had become extremely abusive, both to her and their teenaged daughter. For years the abuse had been verbal. He would yell at her almost daily. Then he began to yell at both the daughter and his wife.

Within the last year he had begun to beat his wife. I could see many times during which she was being yelled at and then a couple of times in which she was actually stricken in the face by her husband, who was in a rage. I could sense the effect this had on the daughter. Her sense of self-worth was extremely low. Being both victim and witness to this excessive domestic violence, she no longer felt like a loved member of this family.

I could tell that this woman had left her husband and was now living in an apartment with her daughter. She was afraid for herself and was also afraid for the daughter. She seemed to fear that the daughter was going to commit suicide.

"Stay close to your daughter," I said to this woman. "I can't quite tell where she is mentally, but she needs your love right now."

"What?" The woman looked puzzled.

I told her what I had seen and then how I had seen it. I told her my whole story. When I had finished, she looked greatly relaxed.

"Please talk to my daughter," she asked. "She needs something hopeful in her life."

I agreed to meet her and her daughter that evening for dinner.

Over dinner, I told the young girl what I had seen that afternoon when I talked to her mother. Now that I was with her, I could tell that the girl was in great personal turmoil. She needed a father figure who loved her, and all she had was a father who seemed to have hair-trigger emotions. It was distressing her. She confessed that she would rather die than go on living with a family like this one.

I told the girl my story.

"Whether it is physical pain or mental pain, it is important to take the long view of things," I said. "Your father's problems won't always be yours. You are young, and you have to hang tough."

Before we spoke more, I excused myself and went to the rest room. That was when everything turned bad.

When I came out, the woman was pinned against the wall by a man who was yelling at her. The daughter was screaming, and the woman's face was a picture of terror.

I moved quickly to get between the woman and this man, who was her estranged husband. A couple of restaurant workers moved in and held the angry husband while the woman and child left.

Later this woman contacted me and told me that the conversation I had had with her daughter had helped the young girl tremendously.

"Now she realizes that he doesn't just hate us, but he hates everybody, himself most of all," she said.

*F*or the most part I have learned how to deal with people who demand my services. Now I do not have a problem saying no to their requests. I realize that I have a great responsibility to others, but an even greater personal responsibility to the evolution of my spiritual self. Now I insist on certain boundaries and have no problem convincing people that they have crossed them.

The early days were different.

A typical day for me amounted to a long session on the living-room couch in which my spirit guides filled me with information that was difficult to comprehend. Friends and acquaintances would drop by during the day to ask for a wide variety of advice, everything from sporting bets to horse races to business advice to their love lives. Some days Sandy would come home to a houseful of people she had never seen before and would never see again. One time she walked in and a visitor turned to her and said, "So what is it you want to ask him?"

At one point she became so frustrated that she suggested I hang a sign that said "Psychic Readings Done Here—$5" with a painting of a giant red palm above it. As I think back over those times, I can't see how she made it so far with me. She is the strongest woman I have ever met and is still one of my best friends.

By then I had met Raymond Moody, the medical doctor who wrote *Life After Life*, the first scientific examination of near-death experiences. He had spoken to dozens of "cases" like me, people who had been to the brink of death. Some of them possessed extrasensory powers. He told me that I was similar to many people out there.

"I wouldn't worry if I were you, Dannion," he said in his gentle way. "Just relax and let things happen. You'll figure out what it all means someday."

"Yeah, right," I said cynically.

Still, what he said proved to be good advice. The problem was that I couldn't relax. Often, sometimes on a daily basis, I was receiving information from the Spirit Beings about my mission on earth. They were giving me information on how to build The Centers. There was no give and take during these meetings with the Spirit Beings. Even though I asked them exactly what I was supposed to do with my intuitive powers, they did not tell me. It was as though they were confirming what Dr. Moody had said to me: "Just relax and let things happen. People who have these experiences often come back with a sense of urgency."

Finally, things did happen. The answer to my prayers walked right in the front door.

Chapter 8

THE MEANING
OF LIFE

*F*or days on end I pondered my situation. I would sit on the sofa and try to answer all of the questions in my mind. I spent hours trying to figure out the particulars of The Centers that the thirteenth spiritual being had told me to build.

I spent more time than I care to remember thinking about the prophecies of the future that the Spirit Beings had revealed to me. There were 117 visions of war, environmental and political change, and technological advances imprinted in my brain. I was shown them only once, and I wrote them in a book that I now keep in a safe place.

When I look at those prophecies, it is like reading headlines from the past twenty years. The only thing is, I was looking ahead in 1975 and these prophecies told me what the events of the next twenty-eight years would be. Why had these been revealed to me? What was I supposed to do with them?

I had many questions in those early days and many questions still. The biggest question, however, was this one: What was I supposed to do with my gift?

If I was sent back for a purpose, as I believed I was, then why was I given an intuitive gift? On one level I thought that I had been given the gift to better understand how we work as spiritual beings. After all, my ability to perceive thoughts showed that I had picked up some extra powers somewhere. Was this some kind of by-product of the lightning strike?

What is the meaning of my life? What is the purpose of life? I frequently wondered. I received no answer from the other side.

*T*hen one day an old man knocked at my door. From my place on the sofa I could see his bent outline against the bright afternoon sun. I could tell that he was wearing a hat, but my poor eyesight prevented me from recognizing the man who would unwittingly change my life.

"Dannion," the man shouted.

The voice was vaguely familiar, but my ability to recognize voices had been temporarily disconnected by the lightning.

"Dannion," the man shouted again. "It's me, Peyser."

"Come in," I shouted, amazed that I had failed to recognize a man I had known since I was a small boy.

In his seventies, Peyser had been shopping at our family grocery store since the days when my grandfather owned it. Peyser's family had its roots in slavery. His father had been born into slavery and had lived most of his life working from dawn to dusk at one of the many plantations in the area during the Civil War era.

Peyser's family owned a farm, which he worked. He once had a second job in town. He saved his money diligently and was able to make sure that his children got good educations. Now they were successful and living outside the state.

I had not seen Peyser for a couple of years, but my father saw him at least once a week at the grocery store. He and my dad were special friends. They spent a lot of time talking about everything from town gossip to the world situation. He even worked out a special deal with my father to donate a certain portion of his grocery bill to his church.

My dad had told me that Peyser had been suffering through an illness for a couple of years now and was having trouble getting around.

When I finally recognized him, I was surprised to see him. I thought he was too sick to get around. I struggled to my feet, and with the help of a cane I shuffled to the door. When he saw me with a cane, he laughed. He was using a cane, too, and the sight of each of us standing there with a third leg was funny to him.

"Old age struck me down, what's your excuse?" he said and laughed.

As we shuffled to the couch, Peyser apologized for not coming to see me sooner. He hadn't been feeling well, he said, but he wanted me to know that I was high on the list of people he was praying for. Now that he saw me in person, he could see that I needed to move higher up on that list of people needing prayer.

"Boy, tell me what happened to you," he demanded.

I told him the whole story. He cringed as I told him about the lightning strike that had caused me to leave my body and had killed me for twenty-eight minutes. Then his face changed as I began to tell him what had happened when I was dead. He looked relaxed and thoughtful as I told him about the crystal cathedrals and the Beings of Light who had educated me about the future and had given me the mission of building Centers when I returned.

Most people looked at me as if I were a nut when I told them that there was more to death than just darkness, but Peyser regarded me with deep understanding.

"So you don't think I'm crazy?" I asked.

"Boy," he said, leaning toward me, "I am smart enough to know that there are many things we don't know."

I felt relief at finally talking to someone who didn't think I had lost my mind. So far the only person I knew who didn't think I was crazy was Dr. Raymond Moody. He was accustomed to stories like mine. It wasn't until the success of his book, *Life After Life*, that people began to understand what had happened to me. Peyser understood right away. My belief that African-Americans in his age group have a deeper spiritual side than other people is rooted in my dealings with Peyser and many of the people he introduced me to in the early days of my search for meaning. They were never disturbed when I talked about my near-death experience. Rather, they listened and responded with interest.

"I've been hearing this stuff since I was a baby," said Peyser.

For the next hour, Peyser told me mystical stories from his own life. Peyser even told me stories about my own family that I had never heard.

For instance, my great uncle Fred, a physician and a state senator for twelve years, told Peyser about a ghost that used to meet him at the top of a hill near a graveyard. As he drove his car over the road, the ghost would appear on the seat next to him. The first time this happened to him was late at night after he had made a number of house calls.

At first he was frightened by the surprise visitor. Then, after it had happened a number of times, he became less frightened. Eventually he came to look forward to his meetings with this ghostly visage. He spoke freely about these apparitional experiences with Peyser, but to my knowledge he never mentioned them to anyone in the family. He never had trouble telling Peyser, though.

"So you see, you aren't the only one in your family who has had contact with the other side."

*P*eyser and I got together often after this first meeting. During his visits, he would come over and tell me things about my family that neither I nor other members of the family knew.

I compared my meetings with Peyser to the panoramic life review that had taken place when I almost died. Through Peyser, who was a deeply spiritual being, I was able to understand who I was and where many aspects of my personality had come from. The fighter in me had clearly come from my grandfather, who owned stores and cafes. Peyser told me about the times when my granddad would storm into a bar fight with no more to protect him than luck and a sawed-off pool cue.

I realized some things during these meetings with Peyser. One was that a life review could take place without having to die. In many ways it was a form of reminiscing. With the help of a friend like Peyser who knew my family and me, I was able to put my life into a perspective that I had never before had. Although having a life review in this fashion was not as dramatic as having a near-death experience, it was still very effective. As I listened to Peyser and his stories about my family and the Old South, I was changed just by knowing about my family roots.

Peyser was very much a part of those roots. Our families had a long history of friendship and business together. As I talked to Peyser I realized that we are all one people. If we could learn to overcome petty differences over color and concentrate on love, which is the true core of our beings, then we could live more happily. I have been asked many times if I saw different racial features in the Beings of Light. The answer is no. Color is not an issue in the afterlife. The core of our being is the bright spiritual light. The light is where we all came from and the light is what we all become.

Whenever I got together with Peyser, his light shown through. Even on days when he was especially uncomfortable from his illness, Peyser had a life glow that exceeded that of healthier people. He was filled with a tranquil peace.

One day I decided to go visit Peyser. I hadn't seen him in about two weeks and had heard through my dad that he was becoming weaker from his illness.

Now it was my turn to stand on his doorstep and call through a screen door at his form lying on the couch. He struggled to his feet, and we had another good laugh at the way in which we shuffled to greet each other.

"The lame leading the lame," he said, pointing to a chair as he made it back to the couch.

I was disturbed by what I saw. Peyser was clearly in bad physical shape. The short walk to the door had drained him of energy, and I could tell that he had lost a lot of weight. I knew that he had been given medication some time before, and I wondered now if the initial round of therapy had failed.

"How are you doing, Peyser?" I asked him. As he thought about the question, I could see images of Peyser's illness in my mind. I was seeing his thoughts, and they were not comfortable ones. I could see his time spent at the doctor's office, and painful procedures being done at the hospital. I could see the lonely hours he spent at home and the sad telephone conversations he had with his children, who were unable to leave their jobs. I could feel other thoughts. How was he going to take care of himself? Where was he going to live?

These are fears that everyone wrestles with at this juncture in their life. I now realize that.

I could see other things too. Peyser was not afraid to die. He had seen his mother and his aunts die and knew that they had seen the same cities of light I had seen. Peyser trusted the spiritual side of life. As he had said to me before, "I am smart enough to know that there are many things we don't know." It was clear to me that Peyser would soon know the spirit world we had talked about so often. I could tell that he had no fear, only pain.

"You know how I'm doing," said Peyser. "It won't be long now."

We sat in silence for several seconds. I was somewhat uncomfortable with other people's deaths in those days. I didn't quite know how to say all of the things that I had learned, so I just sat there and didn't say a thing. Then Peyser said something that changed my life.

"Boy, you have helped me a lot by telling me what you went through," he said. "I always knew that these things were true because my people have always talked about the places you went to. But you are a living person who went there. By talking about them you made my life easier. Boy, you ought to tell other dying people what you know. It sure would make their final days easier."

That's it! What Peyser said was like being struck again by lightning, only this time it brought me to life instead of the brink of death. In a few simple sentences, Peyser had given me the meaning of life. I now knew why I had been blessed with the gift. I now realized what the Beings of Light intended for me to do.

Through Peyser I now knew that I had to use my gift to help people in transition. By using my insights I could cut straight to the heart of the matters that were on the mind of the dying person.

Dying people don't have much time or energy for talk. Yet more than anyone else, they have a deep need to wrap up issues in their lives. By using my psychic abilities to get issues and feelings out in the open, I could help the dying and their loved ones face things that had bothered them for years, and thus heal psychological wounds before their deaths.

As I sat there with my friend Peyser, I knew that his life was ending. At the same time, I knew that mine was just beginning. Peyser had given me an insight that might never have arrived without him. My gift of intuition and my experience of dying was to be passed on to the dying.

*I*ronically, my first hospice case was Peyser.

During the next several days, Peyser took a turn for the worse and decided that he wasn't going to fight any longer.

My father was the first to tell me that Peyser had decided to die. Their relationship had been a good one over the years. Since my dad was closer to Peyser than I was, I was not surprised that he told my dad that he was ready to give up the ghost.

"From now on, we have to deliver groceries to Peyser," said my dad. "He won't be coming down here on his own anymore."

And so it was. I took Peyser under my wing and went to see him as often as possible. In the last two weeks of his life, I was with him frequently. It was there that I began to get in touch with the meaning of life.

I sat at his bedside and we talked. He told me about his children and his sisters. I could see things that he told me play out in my mind, and occasionally I would jump in to fill in the gaps in Peyser's story. I realized that in this situation, I could focus and perceive more precisely than I had been able to up to this point.

As he talked I would see "movies," visuals in my mind that were like short home movies. I would see them and describe my visions to Peyser.

"Boy, you're talking about things that no one outside of my family would know," he would usually say. This would then lead to another line of conversation. Usually the conversations were deeper, since the things I saw were often things that were bothering Peyser. Although he did not want to talk about these things, the fact that I "saw" them and brought them into the open caused him to talk freely about them. It led to a discussion of his hopes and fears that might never have taken place had I not been seeing Peyser's home movie.

I watched him find peace as he talked, and I interjected stories that he had forgotten about his sisters and his children. This was good for Peyser. From these conversations and intuitions Peyser could see that he had done a great job of raising his children. Now he could die with peace of mind, knowing that he was leaving behind children who were a picture of stability. Incidentally, many of his children and grandchildren are working in the nursing home business.

My time with Peyser was when I found out that this perception could help people gain a hold on their spiritual sides. As Peyser saw me picking up things I could not have known without some kind of special intuition, he was at peace with it.

"My people have a history of this stuff," I remember him saying. "We have a knowledge of spirits and people who are in touch with spirits at the time of death. I don't understand all that I know about this, but I do know that this is where it belongs."

*P*eyser's last two days were spent in peace. His family gathered around, and Peyser was able to talk to them with a peace of mind that surprised all of us.

His calmness told me that I had hit on something important in my first hospice case. What had made the difference in Peyser's death was the life review. Our conversations had reviewed the events of his life. My special abilities had allowed us to take a look at his life in depth, without the ego that prevents many of us from talking about our inner feelings. I could see that nothing gives a dying person greater peace than a life review in which the events of his life are put into perspective.

The Meaning of Life

I realized that if a dying person is able to go back over his life in detail, he is able to see things in a different light and may be able to give ground on issues that he was not able to move from before. Even though a person will undergo the process of life review after he dies, the process can help anyone deal with family problems if done before death. Of course, such a review can help the living family members deal with things they may need to bring to a conclusion.

The near-death experience, with its extremely vivid and powerful life review, is something a person goes through alone. We can all do a life review to great benefit, any time at all.

My last conversation with Peyser was about the life review we had gone through together. We talked about the things we had seen together and the benefits he had derived from it. Not only did our life review help him figure out how to divide his property, but it also told him how to express his love to his children in such a way that they would feel fulfilled.

In the end, Peyser was at peace. When I went to see him just before he died, he was thankful for the time we had spent together. There was a joy in him as we talked that his sisters recognized and commented on later. He had found his true self at the end of his life.

I remember his last words to me. "Good-bye," he said. "And don't come tomorrow. I'll be gone."

And he was.

Chapter 9

SPIRITUAL
HOUSE CALLS

Peyser died more than fifteen years ago. In the course of this time, I have performed hospice duty with more than 140 patients. Of those, I have died with nearly forty. In recent years I have become more refined in my dealings with the dying. Looking back on those early days after Peyser, I realize that I was sometimes overzealous. At times I would speak up when I should have remained silent. I would confront family members about the illness of a loved one, or talk to someone about death before they were ready. Sometimes my attempts at spiritual rescue were downright awkward and embarrassing, but I pressed on anyway. As we all know, experience is the best teacher, even if it can sometimes be embarrassing.

One of my early hospice experiences came a few months after Peyser died. This was not the usual sort of experience. I was helping my father in our family grocery store when a regular customer came in, with the weight of sadness on her face.

"What's wrong, Hilda?" I asked.

"My momma's dying," she said.

I knew Hilda's mother and knew that she was well into her nineties. She had been losing her physical strength and mental powers for several years now, and was clearly dying of old age. Now, said Hilda, she was having "hallucinations" of her sisters who had died five years before. "It's terrible," said Hilda. "Sometimes she sits and talks to them all day."

"Maybe it's not so terrible for your mom," I said. I began to tell my own story. I told the whole thing, from the moment I was struck dead by lightning until I was brought back to life by the Spirit Beings.

I then told her about some of the hospice work I had done. At the time I spoke to Hilda, I had been with only a few hospice patients. Still, I knew enough about the deathbed to be able to tell her that it is always surrounded by suffering and gut-wrenching sights, especially for the family. So often there is pain, frailty, emaciation, and many other horrors that make it difficult for even the most loving caregiver to cope.

"But once you get beyond the physical aspects of death, like changing diapers and cleaning people," I said, "you have a chance at an important experience."

"What do you mean?" she asked.

I told her that there are patterns to every death, and that these patterns are the common pathway to spiritual transition. As an old person starts to die, I said, their short-term memory begins to slip. When this happens, events from twenty-five years ago are more easily remembered than what they had for breakfast. Then come hallucinations. Sometimes these hallucinations can be terrifying, I told Hilda, but you have to realize that these are not yet visions of the spirit world, but by-products of the human brain as it dies.

"It becomes obvious when the true visions begin," I told Hilda. She looked puzzled, so I went on to say that the true visions are when the dying begin to see loved ones who have died before them. The presence of these departed loved ones is not frightening. Rather, it is comforting.

"I think this is where the transition takes place," I said to Hilda.

She was puzzled. "What do you mean?"

"At this point, modern medicine stops and the mystical takes over," I explained. "Maybe your mother is taking a glimpse into the spirit world. Maybe she is really talking to her sisters."

Hilda appreciated our conversation. She hugged me and said that everyone else had just said that her mother was going crazy. Now she saw her mother's behavior from a different angle. Now she saw it as normal, possibly even spiritual.

"This will help me look at things in a new light," she said.

Apparently our conversation had been pretty loud, because when I looked up, several of the shoppers in the store were looking at me. My father was standing behind the cash register. He was trying to ignore me, his face practically beet red from embarrassment. Later, when we were alone, he just shook his head.

"Sometimes, you embarrass everybody but yourself.

*T*hat was true then and has been true ever since. Since Peyser helped me figure out the meaning of my life, I have made hundreds of spiritual house calls. I have spent time with the dying, providing them with comfort as they take the most difficult journeys of their mortal lives. I visit these people at home, in hospitals, and in nursing homes. They tell me their stories, and I tell them mine. Through hospice work I have found a "me" that has purpose, one that has truly come to cherish the value of life.

I can vouch for the fact that hospice work helps keep my own small problems in perspective. If you are caring for somebody who weighs seventy pounds as the result of a brain tumor, then you don't have any problems no matter how tough your life is.

I can also vouch for something else. Hospice work is a mystical, even a psychic, experience. Over the years I have realized that by being with people as they make their transitions, I have actually been able to make part of their transitions with them. I have shared visions that the dying are having and have even witnessed important portions of their lives, sharing in their panoramic life reviews as they make their transitions into the spirit world.

*H*ow can this happen?

Much of it has to do with the fact that I have almost died myself. I have been in the exact place where that dying person has been. I know what it is like to be inside a body that has breathed its last breath and is no longer breathing. And I know what it is like to be in a body that breathes its first breath again. Through my own near-death experiences, I have learned how to make the closest contact of all with a person, a dying person in particular.

I do this through color, breath, and fragrance.

In every way, colors and breath are the means by which we can have psychic communication. Breath is the key to spiritual unfolding as well as spiritual understanding. Colors, on the other hand, are waves of light, the smallest common element of which we are all composed.

I realized this when I had my near-death experience. I noticed that everyone had a certain combination of colors around them. As I watched my wife and Tommy as they gave me CPR, for instance, I could see that they had certain shades of colors that the ambulance attendants did not have. They were the same basic colors, they were just shaded differently for each person. When I had my life review, I could see my own colors when I looked at my hands. Once again, the basic colors were the same as those in other people, they were just shaded differently for each person.

I realized at that point that we are all Beings of Light because we are composed of pieces of light. The colors that emanate from us are our individual auras, essentially our celestial signatures.

Through this realization, I have developed techniques that have helped me enhance my ability to be spiritually perceptive.

I have definite methods of doing this. These are methods that anyone can follow to develop extra perception. Some people become immediately and deeply perceptive. Others develop their abilities over a period of time. One thing that always happens is a meaningful bond with the person who is dying.

"As my mother died, I touched her in a way that I had never touched her in all of our life together," wrote one woman who was in the audience at one of my workshops and who followed the techniques I'll soon describe.

"I was able to face her death calmly, which was something she was doing quite well herself," she wrote. "Toward the end, I could sense the presence of spirits coming to get her. These were spirits that she herself could see.

"At the end, I knew when she left her body. I could hear her say good-bye and actually feel something leave her body.

"Up until then I believed that the soul was intangible, if it was anything at all. Now I know there is a soul because I have seen it. My fear of death left me when my mother died. What replaced it was an understanding that we don't know nearly as much as we think we do about what happens after death."

Through trial and error I have developed these techniques for bonding spiritually with hospice patients:

First, I spend hours talking to the dying person. I talk to him about his life, engaging him in a verbal life review. If it's a young person, I will talk to him about physical things like sports or other activities in which he might have been engaged. A young person in a hospice feels confined, and physical activity is usually one of the things missed the most.

With an older person I cover a broader spectrum. Since he has lived through so many changes in society and technology, I will usually ask him how certain modern things differ from the way things used to be.

As we talk, I listen carefully to the person's tone of voice. Voice is as individual as appearance. To my way of thinking, it is the essence of the spiritual body. By imagining his voice as my voice I am able to put myself in his place. It is as though I am listening so intently to his conversation that I almost become him. To do this I clear my mind of anyone in the room but myself and the patient. Doing this puts my ego aside and lets me meld with the other person.

When I am able to do that, my focus shifts to the patient's breathing. Slowly I match his breathing pattern. Then when I am breathing in rhythm with him, I skip a beat and change my pattern. I begin breathing "in" as he breathes "out," and "out" as he is breathing "in." As I do this I imagine a "figure eight" between myself and the patient, in which the air we are breathing out is exchanged in an ebb and flow of energy. At the same time, I place two fingers on his wrist and take his pulse, trying to match my pulse to his. It is amazing how much control we have over our heart rate. I don't know many people who can't just think their pulse faster or slower. It calls for some concentration, but that is my intent.

When I have matched his breathing and heart rate, my focus shifts to the sinus cavities of my own head. I concentrate on filling each of those cavities with air. There are four of these cavities on each side of the face. The way I envision them, they are stacked horizontally, from the forehead to just above the mouth.

To help me concentrate, I think of the air in my various cavities as having color. I start by concentrating on a spot between my eyes, filling it with bright, white light. Then I concentrate on filling each of the eight sinus cavities in my head with the bright white light.

Two at a time, on each side of the face, I fill them with the light. When they are all full, I take a clearing breath that drains them of color. Then I repeat that filling process, concentrating on filling each of my sinus cavities with air that has color. The colors I think of are red, orange, yellow, blue, green, indigo, and violet and shades of the above. As I breathe in and out, I concentrate on filling each of these cavities with rich versions of these colors before clearing them with a draining breath.

I don't for one minute think that the air going into these cavities has color. Rather, the purpose of focusing on these colors is to synchronize something in my brain that allows me to communicate with the dying person. I don't know why this works. Doing this allows the spiritual body to emerge and make itself known. Perhaps that is why focusing on these colors is an important part of my psychic communications with the dying.

Sometimes if I am working with a patient who is truly cognizant, we can make a conscious effort to breathe in unison. That breathing technique— my breathing in while the patient breathes out— has the effect of setting up an ebb and flow between the two of us. Such a rhythm has the effect of making the patient a part of me and me a part of him.

At that point, when I am fully relaxed, I will begin to pick up the patient's thoughts. I have even had it happen in reverse, with him picking up thoughts about me.

You might think that most hospice patients would be opposed to doing something that seems so peculiar as color work and synchronized breathing. In my experience, there has been little resistance.

The hospice experience is not only sometimes frightening for patients, it is also boring and uncomfortable. People in this situation are usually awake and aware, but too sick or distracted to do things to relieve the boredom. As a result they have little to do but stare at the walls and complain about the food. This boredom is not necessarily relieved by family members. When they come in to visit, there is little meaningful talk about anything. The family members and the patient are often in a state of denial, so the subject of death rarely comes up. Instead, there is uncomfortable conversation about some postcard they have received, or hearing how sorry Aunt Jane is that they are ill. Rarely are these conversations very interesting.

Yet most hospice patients want to have meaningful interactions with someone else. Even though people in a hospice are nearing the ends of their lives, they still need to exercise their spiritual and psychological selves. Even the ones who think of these breathing exercises as "New Age foolishness" are willing to try them.

These techniques can open a world of mysticism.

On many occasions I have seen what the dying are seeing and have heard the same celestial music they have heard. This music is like standing in a deep stone canyon and hearing a distant symphony echo off the canyon walls.

A number of times I have even gone with them as they begin their journeys to the other world.

One time, for instance, I was with Albert, a patient who was closer to death than even he knew. We had done breath and color work together for a couple of weeks now, and had become very close. In these last few days as he lay dying, I would come into the room and synchronize my breathing with his, using fragrances to engage all of the senses.

One day when I came in, Albert was staring intently into space. He put his finger to his lips so I would stay quiet and motioned for me to sit down. Faintly, very faintly, I could hear a soothing yet powerful music. We looked at each other in mystery.

"It started last night," said Albert. "I don't know where it's from. It's beautiful, though."

Albert closed his eyes and continued to enjoy the symphony. My eyes widened as I looked around the room. There were no radios in sight, and the television was not on. *Maybe it is coming from another room,* I thought. I stuck my head into the hallway and listened. There was no music, just the sounds of people rustling around and getting up for the day. I walked slowly down the hall and listened, from door to door. There was no music in the entire wing.

"Can you come with me a minute?" I asked a passing nurse.

I escorted her into Albert's room and asked her to stand very still.

"Do you hear it?" I asked.

She listened a moment and then shook her head. "Hear what?" she asked.

Albert chuckled. "It's just music for you and me," he said. "We're the only ones who can hear it."

I sat in silence with Albert as we listened to the music. I was puzzled by the source of the music until I looked at Albert's face. It was as serene as a sleeping child's. Then it hit me. *The music is coming from the spirit side,* I said to myself. *They will be coming soon to take Albert.*

Another day passed and then another. The two of us sat almost in silence as the music played on and on. By the evening of the second day, Albert was fading as peacefully as I have ever seen anyone fade. He opened his eyes once more and motioned me to his side with a flick of his wrist.

"I'm going with the music," he said.

Within five minutes he was gone.

*F*ew deathbed scenes are as peaceful as Albert's. Usually there is a fair amount of chaos around a dying person. Nurses are going in and out of the room, family members are weeping and begging for medical and divine intervention, and doctors are doing what they can to make the person pain free.

In the midst of all this confusion there is still the opportunity for psychic experience, which I define as the sharing of another person's reality from inside his mind. When this happens, there is benefit to everyone at the deathbed.

For the living there is comfort in knowing for sure that a loved one has passed into a welcoming environment. There is also awe in experiencing a world that was previously outside their five senses.

For the dying there is the comfort of having a loved one who is not trying to tell him he will be okay. From this basis of truth, they form a bond that allows them both to pass at least momentarily into the next world.

I have seen other people coming to greet the dying on a number of occasions. Most of the time it comes like a faint light silhouette of a person coming across the room. Other times I don't see anything that definite. Rather, I will just see something occupying a space in the room.

For example, I was with a woman whose husband was a scientist and not open to talking about spiritual matters. She had asked to speak to me because she needed a sympathetic ear.

"When my mother died," she told me, "she came to visit me in spirit form. She stood in front of me in the living room and told me that she would always be with me. When I have talked about this with my husband, he gets very uncomfortable."

We talked about that incident for a while until I asked a question that got to the real reason she wanted to talk to me. "Has this happened again?"

"Yes!" she replied excitedly. "My mother has come back to me again."

As we talked about these sightings, I could see that the woman was happy about what had happened. She had been in a lot of pain, and, frankly, the return of her mother meant that her pain would soon be over.

Two days later I returned to see her. She was nearly dead now, and there was little I could do but sit with her and her husband and wait for death.

Suddenly, she opened her eyes and started breathing faster. At the base of the bed, a yellowish light appeared. Both the husband and I saw it. We watched as it moved toward the woman. As it reached the side of her bed, it slowly disappeared. When it was gone, the woman died.

Another time I was with a man and his wife at their home near Atlanta. He was dying, and she needed help attending to all the difficult tasks that surround the deathbed.

As the hour of his death approached, we sat next to his bed. This man, his name was Henry, was in his seventies and his wife, Elisa, was maybe ten years older than he was. It was a touching scene watching these two together for the last time. They had been married for at least forty years, and in a very short period of time, death would separate them.

We sat in relative silence. She swabbed her husband's lips with water and spoke comforting words to him, but that was all the noise there was in the room. We were not talking about angels, or Beings of Light, or anything of the sort. We were being quiet.

Suddenly Henry's eyes got as big as saucers. "Mother's coming, Mother's coming," he said.

Elisa and I looked across the room. There was an energy forming like heat waves from a blacktop highway during summer. At first it was vague, but as we watched, it developed more substance until it had a silky form.

"I guess that's what he is talking about," said Elisa. "That must be his mother."

The form hovered there for a long time before it faded away. Even though I have seen this or similar spirits on a number of occasions, I was speechless. Frankly, there are no words that can adequately describe the wonderment of this experience.

The same was true of my mother, Margie, who died in 1984 of lupus and Raynaud's disease, a circulatory problem.

As her problems worsened, she was subjected to some painful and unnecessary surgery on her lungs. A few days after the surgery, I was visiting my mother in her hospital room when she told me of a visit made by a spirit.

"Dannion," she said, her voice a whisper. "Let it stop now. Marion has come. I know it is okay to die."

It has happened, I thought. As I held my mother's hand, I thought about the story of Marion. She was my mother's younger sister. When she was only fifteen years old, Marion fell out of the school bus and was crushed and killed beneath its wheels. They were the closest of friends.

Now, after all these years, my mother was telling me about Marion appearing in her room. She had come back to help my mother die.

Who better to come for Mother than Marion? I thought as I listened to Mom tell her story. *No one could do it better.*

It was a beautiful moment, an island of light in a sea of bleakness for the Brinkley family. Up until that point we were considering irrational ways to prolong her life. More surgery and stronger medications were being considered, only because we were fighting the notion that our matriarch was dying.

With the arrival of Marion, however, the mood changed. We began to prepare for Mom's death. We told the doctors that there would be no more intervention to save her life. How could there be? Marion had come.

As the family sat by her bed, we reflected on all the things my mother had taught us. She was a tough and good mother, and a little neurotic on top of it all. She had no trouble pulling those three traits together to discipline me when I needed it. I had not been a good child. I was always in trouble and always more interested in fighting with the other kids than in making friends with them. I was a bully, to be sure, but I never even tried to act tough to my mother. She was the teacher in the family, and I was one of her students. She was determined to teach me about life, like it or not.

As her three children sat at her deathbed, we told stories from our childhood that made all of us laugh. We reviewed our lives together and put everything in order. As we did this, the deathbed scene became less hectic and more placid. In that sense we were all at peace with what was happening.

After seeing Marion, Mother taught me her final lesson. She died with peace and dignity, with all of her ducks in a row.

*B*eing at a deathbed, and sometimes seeing these spirits in the room, are the most mystical moments of my life. The awareness of love. The feelings of joy and peace. The comfort of knowing that I am helping somebody at a troubled time. The security and knowledge that there is a spiritual system that takes you from this world to the next world. These qualities make these moments so mystical.

Proudly I have these experiences using techniques I have developed to enhance my hospice ability. I have refined them over the years, but they all spring from the fact that I have essentially been dead twice and know what it is like to both lose and gain the breath of life.

Any hospice worker can take part in such mystical experiences. One of the best examples of health care workers sharing a dying experience comes not from me but from a study conducted by the American Parapsychological Association in which 640 doctors and nurses were asked about mystical events that take place around the deathbed.

One of the cases involved a patient in his forties who had known the nurse who was attending him for many years. On the day of his death, this nurse and others were spending time at his bedside, praying and talking to him. The event she described makes a persuasive case for the reality of the paranormal:

"He was unsedated, fully conscious, and had a low temperature. He was a rather religious person and believed in life after death. We expected him to die, and he probably did, too, as he was asking us to pray for him. In the room where he was lying, there was a staircase leading to a second floor. Suddenly he exclaimed: 'See, the angels are coming down the stairs. The glass has fallen and broken.' All of us in the room looked toward the staircase where a drinking glass had been placed

on one of its steps. As we looked, we saw the glass
break into a thousand pieces without any apparent
cause. It did not fall; it simply exploded. The
angels, of course, we did not see. A happy and
peaceful expression came over the patient's face
and the next moment he expired. Even after his
death the serene, peaceful expression remained on
his face."

I don't know if these health care workers were
breathing in sync with this patient or if they were
concentrating on colors being breathed into their
sinus passages.

I believe that this experience shows there is
some substance to the spirit world, at least enough
to shatter a glass so that all could see. If such an
experience could happen to health care workers
who were not even trying, then imagine what
could happen to those who really wanted an experience.

I have given these techniques to hospice workers and have seen them get the same results. Once
they learn to overcome the horrible physical
aspects of dealing with the dying, they have the
opportunity to open up their higher conscious-
nesses. By helping dying people have a life review,
and by using the techniques I have described in
these pages to connect with the dying on a psychic level, hospice workers can discover aspects of
themselves that they did not know existed.

Through that, they can make the paranormal a normal part of their lives and better understand the mystery inside each of us.

Chapter 10

THE SPIRITUAL PAYCHECK

*M*y main mission right now is to die with people. One of the greatest problems is our fear of death. It is this fear—brought about by our misperception of death—that causes millions of people to die alone each year. I think this is a sin, not to mention a missed opportunity for spiritual growth.

When I mention that I am "dying" with someone, I usually get a strange look. I don't mean that I am literally dying with the person. Everyone dies or makes the transition alone and in his own way, just as we all grieve and deal with trauma in our own way.

By helping people make the transition into the next world, I function as a spiritual companion. I come together with the dying person at least a couple of hours a week. If he is too tired, sick, or angry to talk, I just stay with him and take care of whatever physical needs he might have.

The only thing I am inflexible about is leaving. Even if someone tells me to get out of the room, I stay right there. "You can stare at the wall for an hour," I tell the stubborn ones. "But I am not leaving until your time is up."

Eventually everyone does want to talk. A very sick person may start out by ignoring me, or calling me names like "the grim reaper." Persistence usually pays off, though. After about three visits there is a look in the dying person's eyes that tells me I am welcome.

That is when "dying with someone" really begins.

It is also when we the living begin to understand the notion that we are mighty *spiritual* beings, not just *human* beings. At that point the earthly problems around us become less important. We are not nagged by bad jobs or tormented by the petty annoyances in life that seem like such big problems. By dying with someone you see that your spiritual nature is alive and well. You gradually lose your fear of death. At the same time, your joy of living increases.

By the way, all of these benefits come from people who can't give you anything for your time but love and need. As I tell so many people, "Working in a hospice pays off. It may not pay off here in the mortal world, but in the spiritual sense, the retirement program is out of this world."

As this is written I am dying with three very different people under three very different sets of circumstances. One is a former grocer with a brain tumor who was maudlin and frightened of death when I first met her. Now she laughs even though she still has fears.

The second is a middle-aged man with lung cancer who is seeing spirits in his room. Their presence frightened him at first, but I showed him how to work with them. Now he welcomes them like friends and knows that they will be with him when he dies.

The third is an eighty-year-old woman whose heart has been slowly failing since she had a heart attack five years ago. I met her when she was dying from pneumonia. As a heart patient myself, I can relate to pain in the chest that takes your breath away. I dropped in on her one day to tell her what I knew about heart trouble and also about death. She invited me back to hear more of these strangely comforting tales. Now she no longer fears death. She is excited about leaving a not very useful body but has rebounded to the point where she is a part-time receptionist, answering the telephone at the nursing home.

Let me introduce you to some of the people who give me my spiritual paycheck.

*H*elen was in her seventies when her doctor discovered that a brain tumor was the cause of her headaches. Her first reaction upon hearing the news was to ask, "Is there no rest for the weary?"

She then returned to her tiny grocery store and worked for the rest of the day.

It was a hard thing to do, but Helen was a tough woman. Since her husband died, she had managed the store alone. Besides the daily grind of doing the books, cleaning, stocking shelves, and managing the cash register, Helen had the hard task of collecting payments from those to whom she extended credit.

Over the next several months, surgeries to get rid of the tumor took their toll. She became weaker and weaker, until she was able to run the store only from a wheelchair. Unable to care for herself any longer, Helen finally moved into a nursing home.

That is when I met her. Her daughter wanted me to talk to her mom. "She is so depressed that she won't even look at me," said the daughter. "She is angry and acts like she is letting us down. We don't want her to die like this."

I stopped by to see her. "Hi, I'm Dannion Brinkley," I said. For a moment I thought she was having some kind of seizure. She just stared straight ahead at the ceiling and said nothing. It was as though I didn't even exist. After a few moments, though, I could tell that she was just ignoring me. Helen wanted to be left alone.

Other people may have taken offense, but not me. I know what it is to resent mortality, and certainly know how painful illness is.

"I'll just sit here," I said. That is what I did on that first day, just sat in silence.

The second day was not much better, nor was the third. On the fourth day, I changed my approach. I brought a hospice volunteer into the room with me and told Helen that I was training him. I explained the physical aspects of helping a patient like Helen, who was unable to walk or even turn over in bed. As I did this, I pretended that Helen didn't care that we were in the room.

"Thanks for letting us come in," I said as we started to leave.

She motioned me over. "Come on back and we'll talk," she said.

When I came back later we talked about the grocery business. Since my family has been in the grocery business for more than a hundred years in South Carolina, we had a lot to say. After covering this common ground, Helen began to talk about her illness.

"I know I am going to die, but no one will talk to me about it," she said. "Even the doctor says that there might be hope, but I can see in his eyes that he doesn't really believe it. Why can't they just tell me the truth?"

"Not many people can talk about death because they think it is horrible," I said. "I've been there, and I look at it in more positive terms."

I told her my story from beginning to end, including the stories of many of the people I had encountered over the years who had been on the brink of death like I had been. I gave her the specifics of the dying experience, how she would go up a tunnel into a place of great beauty and be greeted by someone she knew or magnificent Beings of Light. Some of them would be new to her, but others would be friends and relatives who had died before her. This is what other people have told me. I was greeted only by Spirit Beings I didn't recognize. "To give you an idea of the type of person I was, the two times I died I didn't see any of my relatives, even my mother," I said. "I guess no one up there who knew me wanted to see me again, but if I had seen my mom, I may never have come back."

Then I told her about the life review, and how she would live her life again in the blink of an eye. This time, though, she would know how everything she had done had affected the people in her life.

"This is what we can work on now," I said. "You are going to have this panoramic life review when you die. Let's talk about your life and explore what that review will be like."

From then on, our conversations changed. She knew I wasn't going to lie to her about her chances of surviving this brain cancer. By facing her illness, we got over a huge stumbling block and became friends in truth. When that happened, we talked about love and her family life. We discussed the hopes and dreams that had come true, as well as the failures and disappointments. For several hours a day, we lived her life in reverse.

The panoramic life review is more than just your own home movie. A person who has such a life review is feeling what he meant to people and how he influenced events. A person not only sees what he has done to another person, for instance, but also knows firsthand how that person felt. A whole chain reaction of feelings may be experienced, as well as an awareness of how their reaction to a person affects that person's reaction to others, and so on.

It is the life review that has the greatest effect on people who have had near-death experiences. Although passing up a tunnel, seeing dead relatives, and being bathed in the mystical light all have a great effect, the panoramic life review instills in people a sense of who they are and how they fit in. The life review will let us see everything we have done and become everyone we have ever met. It also give us a true understanding of justice and equality. During the experience, you become the judge and jury over events in your own life.

"Through that experience," I said to Helen, "you will know just how it is that you have affected the world."

All of this was a great relief for Helen. Although she continued to get sicker, her attitude improved. She still had anger about dying, but it did not fester as it had before we began to talk.

One of the best things that happened as I dealt with Helen was a telephone call I received from her daughter. "I went to see her today and she laughed like I haven't seen her laugh since I was a child," she said.

I have eased Helen's mind about her fate and

have made her last days on earth more pleasurable, but it is a two-way street. While she is taking much of my love with her, I am keeping much of hers with me. By dying with someone, you are both nourished.

*E*very hospice patient has different needs. Given enough time, the patient will tell you what those needs are. That has been the case with Raleigh, who was dying of lung cancer that had spread to his brain.

Raleigh, like so many other hospice patients, didn't want to deal with the subject of death. Even though he knew he was in a hospice program, he didn't want to face the fact that he was not going to be alive much longer.

Every time a nurse came into the room, Raleigh would remind her that he was a code three, which meant that if he went into cardiac arrest they were to wheel in a crash cart and try to revive him.

"Go in and talk to Raleigh," one of the nurses said. "He is so afraid that I can hardly deal with him."

I went by his room. "How are you doing?" I asked, sticking my head in the door.

"Fine," he said.

After several days of this, the look in Raleigh's eyes changed. Need replaced the wall of denial that I had seen on previous days. "I've been waiting for you," he said. "Can we talk?"

The Spiritual Paycheck

For the next hour we talked about death, a subject that Raleigh had discussed with no one. He asked what happened when we die, and I told him my personal story, leading up to the part where I was taken to the crystal city of light. I described this place of massive spiritual power, with cathedrals of crystal glass that glowed from within. I described sitting inside one of these cathedrals and gazing in awe at a spectacular white podium at the front of the room that stood out in stark contrast to the carousel of colors that merged and surged on the wall behind.

"Suddenly, the podium was filled with Beings of Light," I said. "They were the most magnificent things I had ever seen, and they radiated a glow that was both kindly and wise."

He stopped me right there.

"I have been seeing Beings too," he told me. "At first I was scared, but I can tell that they don't mean any harm. Now I see them in the room with me a couple of times a day. Are these the same things you saw in the spirit world?"

I told him the truth. Brain cancer can cause hallucinations, but usually they are frightening or confusing.

"If what you are seeing seems to be helpful, then maybe it's the real thing," I told Raleigh. "Maybe someone is coming to help you make that transition."

We talked some more, and during the next few days there was a tremendous change in Raleigh.

His fear of death diminished greatly, and he was no longer concerned about the Beings that only he could see. He told his doctor that he could face his death without fear. Soon he demonstrated it by reducing his medical orders to a code one, which meant no resuscitation was required. He had begun to control his life at a time when most people lose control.

He is much calmer these days, and in less pain too. As his circle of life closes, Raleigh has made peace with himself, and as a result is much less fearful.

*S*urvival is not the measure of success in hospice work, but it is wonderful when it happens. For Bonnie it means that she will be with us for a few more prosperous and happy years. I think it is all because she lost her fear of death.

Bonnie is a patient at one of the nursing homes where I visit. She was healthy until her seventies, when she had a heart attack. Since then, she had lost much of her energy and, with it, her will to live. Over the course of several months, she became extremely depressed and increasingly bedridden. Finally she developed a touch of pneumonia and refused to eat. "It's time to die," she announced to one of the nurses.

At that point, the nurse contacted me.

When I poked my head into Bonnie's room, she laughed. "They say that death is sure to follow a visit from Dannion Brinkley," she said. "So come on in."

I held Bonnie's hand and could tell that she was not dying from the disease, but the loss of vitality that it represented. The chest pains slowed her down, and her weakened heart muscle sapped her energy. For the first time in her life, Bonnie didn't have the physical strength to keep up with all the things she wanted to do. She had become depressed and then came down with pneumonia. Now she said she was ready to die.

But she really didn't mean it.

As I began the breathing technique and held her hand, I closed my eyes and began to see snippets of her life as though I was watching Bonnie's home movies in my head. Intuitive abilities are a gift given to many people who have near-death experiences. These "extra" abilities have been well-documented in fine research done by scientists like Dr. Melvin Morse, author of *Closer to the Light,* and Dr. Kenneth Ring, author of *Heading Toward Omega.* These abilities manifest themselves in different ways with different people. For me, I see what I call "home movies" when I touch someone, and that is what happened on this day with Bonnie.

"I don't think you want to die at all," I suggested after watching her movie.

We talked about what I had seen, which led to discussing aspects of her life that I had not seen. She told me how disappointed she was at not being able to get around much anymore. I told her that a restricted life could still be satisfying enough to want to stay alive. I knew that was true because I was living under just such restrictions.

She told me that she was frightened when I showed up. She said the joke around the nursing home was that I was one of the signs of impending death. "Just what do you tell people that makes them die so fast?" she asked me.

"I try to take the terror out of death," I said. We talked about spiritual experiences and the amazing things that happen when we die. I told her how surprised I was to find that our consciousness was not extinguished at death, and described for her the things I had seen and experienced as a dead person.

I came back to see Bonnie over the next several days. Instead of getting sicker as most of my hospice patients do, Bonnie got better. Her pneumonia turned into a cough and then disappeared altogether.

This was less than a year ago. Now I joke that Bonnie has taken over the nursing home where she lives. She answers the telephone at the reception desk and directs people who come in to see family members. She now feels certain that she will live longer, but is not afraid of death if it comes sooner. "When the time comes, I'll be glad to be rid of this body," she says. "Floating around sounds good to me."

The most important thing with Bonnie is not that she is alive, but that she is glad to be alive.

The Spiritual Paycheck

The stories of people who see the spiritual world after having near-death experiences increases people's desire to live much more than it does their desire to die. I have seen this many times, but a number of medical researchers have actually proved it. In some of their studies, people who attempt to commit suicide are given literature to read about the near-death experience. After just reading about these experiences, those who have attempted to commit suicide are unlikely to try it again, while those who have not read about them are fifty to a hundred times more likely to try suicide again than those who have never tried it.

There are a number of theories about why this is so. One noted researcher feels that there is a discharge of destructive energies during a near-death experience that may affect those who even just know about them. Another believes that increased spiritual knowledge may enhance a patient's self-image and self-esteem.

I don't doubt any of these theories, but to them I have to add one of my own. I think the knowledge imparted through the near-death experience reduces not only our fear of death, but also our fear of life. By exploring the spiritual adventures of those who have almost died, the despair of living is replaced by a belief that life goes on, even after we have left these "fossilized" bodies.

$\mathcal{I}$ find the time I spend in hospice work to be tremendously comforting. I recommend it to everybody. With the fact that seventy-six million baby boomers could find themselves in the position of being caregivers, it is important to prepare as soon as possible. It is in these final moments of a person's life, when there is no ego left and no pretense to overcome, that true love shines through, for the caregiver and the cared for.

It is in a hospice where I take my stand against the skeptics who define us as soulless pieces of meat, nothing more than neurons and chemical reactions. There is no way that a person can spend time with the dying and consider their final moments to be wishful dreams caused by the fear of extinction. At no time have I found that humans reveal more of their spiritual underpinnings than in hospice work. When someone can entrust in you her fears and anxieties and you can attempt to understand those fears and help her make the transition, then you are experiencing a love and humanity that defines you as a spiritual being.

Chapter 11

A CHECK
TO BE CASHED

I did a lot of my hospice work with AIDS patients in the early days of the epidemic. They were the unwanted patients, and remain so to this day. Although we now have more compassion for people with this tragic disease, they are still treated much like the lepers who were outcasts in the time of Jesus. There are even many doctors who will not work with those who have the AIDS virus for fear of getting it themselves.

I was drawn to AIDS patients from the beginning by Franklyn Smith, a pioneer in the use of guided imagery in hospice and AIDS care. In part I felt that those who truly needed hospice care were the ones who society had turned its back on. As they became sicker, they also faced the fear of being deserted by family and church. I knew that they needed my help the most.

It was through AIDS victims that I discovered the value of the life review.

The near-death experience made me realize that I am part of the woven tapestry of life. When a corner of the cloth is given a tug, the whole thing moves. The power of such a life review is that it lets you know what your place is in the universe, it helps you see who you truly are. You are alone, yet more a part of humanity than ever before. As Ralph Waldo Emerson said, "Nothing can bring you peace but yourself."

So many AIDS patients have no one but themselves. They are abandoned and sometimes ostracized by family and friends. If they are going to find peace in their dying days, they are forced to find it alone.

AIDS victims are generally more reflective than many other hospice patients. They are younger and are filled with disappointment about the life they are missing. If they have contracted the disease through a homosexual lifestyle, they often carry a lot of mental baggage that adds to their physical pain. Those dying of AIDS tend to become very philosophical.

One of these was a patient named James. He was in the last few days of his life and was exhibiting all the external signs of a disease that was literally eating his insides. His skin was a patchwork of bruises and sores from blood vessel cancer, and his breathing was labored from the pneumonia that was robbing him of lung space. He was dying before my very eyes, yet it was not his physical condition that concerned him right then. He was worried about tying up loose ends in his life. He did not want to die with the knowledge that he had not done everything he could to make his short life as good as it could be.

He told me about his relationship with his father. He was a harsh man with whom James had never felt comfortable. No matter what he did as a child, it was criticized by his father. James worked hard at his grades and even excelled at football, but it was never enough to make his father happy. Finally he realized that it wasn't *what* he was doing that bothered his father, it was the person he was.

"I was different, and my dad knew it," said James.

That realization only made things worse between James and his father. Their relationship began to darken. They had violent disagreements and even physical fights. These fights were always about something minor. They never dealt with James's being gay, which was the real issue between the two men.

After James finished high school, he had very little to do with his father. If it hadn't been for visits to his mother, he would never have seen his dad again. As it was, they rarely spoke with civility toward one another.

Now, as he was facing the end of his life, he wanted to speak frankly with his father about who he was. Even though he knew they could never be true friends, he wanted to at least try to put those years of animosity behind them.

He did not believe such a healing would ever happen. His parents didn't even know he was in the hospital, let alone that he would soon die from AIDS. How could he tell them now? How could he possibly let them see him this way?

"If they see me this way, they will die before me," he said and laughed. "My folks couldn't take that kind of shock."

We spoke about his relationship with his parents and about his life in general. As we spoke it was clear that James was reviewing his life in much the way that he probably would during his dying experience. He was not ashamed of his lifestyle. "That is the way I was made, the way it was supposed to be for me," he said.

He was sorry about all the anger that had been spent between him and his father. Since he had made a conscious decision not to contact his parents, he was resigned to the fact that he would die with their relationship still an open wound.

"Life is the same for everyone," he said one day with a certain amount of bemusement. "No matter who we are, we have all written a check and are now just waiting for it to be cashed."

*W*hen I deal with the dying, I realize just how true that is. When they begin to recount their lives, I am reminded of an accountant at his ledger book, tallying up profit and loss. They account for all the bad things that they can remember and counter it with all of the good.

By the end, they almost always have to write some kind of emotional check, sometimes for a fairly hefty sum.

One such check was written by an AIDS patient named John. He was only twenty-four years old when he discovered that he was HIV positive. When I met him in a hospice program in Charleston, South Carolina, he had begun to develop pneumonia and was losing weight at an alarming rate. On top of that, he became violently ill when he took the medications that he needed in order to stay alive one more day.

Despite the severity of his illness, he had not resigned himself to death the way so many people have. When I first walked into his room, he had the panicked look of someone who was very afraid to die. I have always likened that to the look a mountain climber must have on his face when his rope breaks and he knows the end is just a fast drop away.

"Why me?" he asked as I sat down. "What have I done to deserve this?"

Before I could speak, he began to guess as to why this plague had been visited on him. He had been raised in a deeply fundamentalist religion that preached hellfire and damnation for those who deviated from the teachings of the church. His lifestyle changed greatly after leaving the small Southern town of his birth. It was the "sins" he had committed as a homosexual that now caused this physical suffering. "I earned AIDS," he said, and then he began to sob.

Many hospice workers cannot handle scenes like this one. I have seen veteran hospice people leave a patient's room at this point, sometimes without even saying anything. They cannot stand the pain in a person's voice as he faces his pending extinction, and they don't quite know what to say. I hope this book will help in that situation.

For me it is different. Although I empathize with the way these patients feel, I cannot sympathize with them. I have been through this twice myself, and if I learned anything it is that we deliver our own judgment through our life review. We are our harshest critics, without a doubt. One of the greatest gifts of the life review is that it is a pure experience of empathy. Of everyone I have met who had a near-death experience, the judgment they have cast on themselves as a result of the life review is as tough as any that could be handed out by someone else.

"I was ashamed at the way I had treated people," said one man I talked to who had a life review as a result of a heart attack. "If I could have, I would have sentenced myself to hell."

I agreed. If there had been a hell, I certainly would have been sent there after my first life review. My background was as tainted and deserving of a visit to such a place as any you could find. Even at that, I found myself surrounded by a love so great that I was forgiven even though I could not forgive myself. I have tried to live up to that love ever since.

Still, it is hard to convince someone who is dying physically and is in agony mentally that a better time will come after death. At times it is even harder to convince someone that he must learn to forgive himself so that love can enter into his life. With John, all I could do was tell him what I knew would happen.

"All of us have these fears of death," I told him. "All of us are going to die. What is happening to you is more intense than most people, because you are young and dying of an incurable disease. But all people who are dying ask the same question: Why is this happening to me?"

I sat in silence until John calmed down. Then I began to tell him everything I could about the experience of death. Although I could not guarantee that these things would happen, I did tell John that most people who have the so-called "near-death experience" describe it in the same way.

Just hearing about the dying experience calmed John. It gave him hope, which is a handle we can all grip.

"Now let's practice for your life review," I said. "Let's talk about the good things in your life, the things you are proud of. After that, we'll talk about the bad things too. Together we will draw an overview of your life, of all your hopes and dreams."

I have seen life reviews change the most guilt-ridden of hospice patients. By being allowed to glimpse their spiritual natures—the way in which they have co-created with God—I have seen the terror disappear from a dying person's life.

*T*im was one such patient. He, too, was dying of AIDS, and like so many others he was spending his final days damning himself for his lifestyle.

"If I wasn't gay, I wouldn't be sick," he said.

"But you didn't know about this disease," I said. "No one knew about it until they got it and then they didn't even know what it was."

"Do you think this is a message from God? A plague on gay people?"

"Tim," I said, using my most understanding voice, "if it were a plague on gays, then only gays would have it. Innocent children and old people who aren't gay have this disease. It's just a disease spread through blood, that's all. It's not a message."

I don't think Tim believed that it was just a disease. Tim expressed a very lopsided view of his life. Day after day he brought up bad things from his past, never discussing the good things that were surely there. To hear Tim tell it, his was a grim and evil existence. "Tell me about the good things in your life too," I begged. He wouldn't. By Tim's own account, he was a person without redemption.

As the illness took hold, there were so many complications that any medical intervention was like trying to stop holes in a leaky dike. There were brain tumors, pneumonia, cancers, and things I don't even know how to name, all of which made Tim sicker and sicker.

One day when I wasn't there, he went into cardiac arrest. The doctor on call stood over him for a moment and then out of instinct tried to restart his heart. He gave him closed chest massage and, to his surprise, Tim's heart started beating again.

I heard about Tim's revival that night, and the next day I went to see him. He was still very near death, but his attitude had changed entirely. Because of what had happened the night before, he had seen good things about himself, he said, and no longer had such a great fear of death.

"I could hardly breathe, so I pressed my call button to get a nurse to the room. Then I felt this huge pressure in my chest and I blacked out. I think I was dead at that point.

"The next thing I knew, I could see the back of the doctor as he pushed on my chest and I thought that he was just wasting his time. I was sure I was dead. I could hear music, and I was going into a tunnel, and there was no way I was coming back.

"I went into a light and I saw my life. I saw the bad things I talked to you about, but they didn't seem so bad this time. I also saw many of the times in my life where I had done good things for other people. I saw the things I had done for my sister, who had a difficult childhood. I made her life better by helping her through rough emotional periods. I could feel the way it made me feel when I was helping her, but best of all I could feel the way it made her feel."

As Tim talked I could see that his life review had helped him rebuild what was left of his life. He had gone from being horrified and guilty to being at peace with himself. His life review had helped him see the spiritual nature of all of his acts. Rather than fearing eternal damnation, Tim could see that there were many acts of kindness in his own life that he had ignored, acts that mean even more on the other side than they do on this one. He now had a great sense of peace.

He talked openly about his problems and his personality without being caught up in what others thought of him. He had a short remission after this near-death experience and used his remaining strength to write notes to family and friends. This was his effort to tie up loose ends and communicate with loved ones one final time.

He let me read some of those notes. They were all filled with sorrow at having to die so soon. But some of them had their share of humor too. "I always thought I would live forever," he wrote to his sister. "But I guess I'm going to live just a few years longer than our family dog."

In all of his letters he referred to things from the past, sometimes events he had seen in a new light through his near-death experience. This happens frequently to near-death experiencers. He was not just mulling these over aimlessly, his remembrances were filled with resolve. "Most of the time I intended to do good things," he wrote to a friend. "After what happened this last week (his near-death experience) I now know that intention counts for an awful lot in life."

On an almost daily basis I consciously have a life review. This doesn't mean that the life review I have is the intense variety I had during my two death experiences. What I do to have a life review is reflect on my daily actions. By having this sort of pre-death life review, I am able to strip away the ego, through which so many of us filter our actions, and look honestly at who I am.

I often joke that we are having a near-death experience right now because we are living our life review right now. That makes the life review the most obvious aspect of the near-death experience to use in building your empathy, sensitivity, and direction on a daily basis.

It also means that we don't have to wait until we die to receive the benefits of life review. As I pointed out in the last chapter, I meditate on my life almost daily. It helps me function as my own judge and jury.

The concept that we are our own judges is a difficult one for most people to grasp. In the Western world, many have come to believe that God will preside over our eternal fate, sitting like a judge on the bench, deciding if we are good enough to join him in heaven or are so bad that we warrant an eternity in hell. For some there is even a place called purgatory, a sort of middle realm that some religions believe is set aside for those who get a hung jury.

This has not been my experience either time I died. Neither time did I find myself in any kind of celestial courtroom attempting to defend my life. What went on both times was actually worse. I found that I sat in judgment on myself. I did not receive a stern rebuke from the Being of Light, which initiated my life review. Instead I felt the love and joy that a wise grandfather might radiate to a grandchild who has not yet gained the wisdom of long life. "You are the difference that God makes," the Being of Light communicated to me. "And that difference is love."

The Being was then quiet. With gentle and loving support to back me up, I was allowed a period of reflection on my own life, the life I had just witnessed from all possible sides.

I took important questions away with me: Had I given as much love as I had taken? Did I practice random acts of kindness? Was I responsible for making people feel good just for the sake of feeling good? These were the things on which I reflected.

A Check to Be Cashed

The Being of Light provided the forum for my judgment by allowing me to have a life review. I judged myself, a far more painful process considering that you really cannot lie to yourself. As you read this, think about how much you truly know about yourself, and how stern you would be if you had to judge yourself.

The Being of Light stood by and kindly told me the meaning of life: "Humans are powerful spiritual beings meant to create good on the earth," he said. "This good isn't usually accomplished in bold actions, but in singular acts of kindness between people."

The Being told me that it was "the little things that count" because they show who you truly are. I realize now that small acts of kindness are spontaneous acts, almost like reflexes. When you buy a homeless person a meal or offer assistance to a friend in need, you do it with no agenda. Help like that truly comes from the bottom of your heart. Help like that is true love.

I have heard nearly the same message from hundreds of others who have had near-death experiences. These people were lucky enough to survive their glimpses of the afterlife. They, too, had life reviews and received counseling from a Being of Light. The revelations they received were almost identical to mine.

Here are some of the messages I have heard

from people who have had near-death experiences:

"I now know that there is a piece of God in each of us that is nothing more than kindness. We are supposed to spread that piece of God around."

"I now know that death is nothing to worry about. What we should be worrying about is how we act toward other people."

"I realized that time as we see it on the clock isn't how time really is. What we think of as a long time is really only a fraction of a second. Thinking like that has really made me less materialistic."

"I learned that there is a universe out there, but there is one in here too (pointing toward heart). We are all part of the same universe. If we hurt someone else, we hurt ourselves too. It is just that simple."

"I learned that objects in our life are meaningless and unimportant. It is the spirit world that is important. Jewelry and fancy homes have no real value. We should judge ourselves through our good deeds."

I find it revealing that people are not coming back from these celestial life reviews with cures for cancer or solutions to our planet's overpopulation. Rather, they are coming back with a message of love, caring, and concern for their fellow man. Apparently, this is information that those in the spiritual realm deem pertinent to the human race. That is the information that is imparted to us on the day we judge ourselves.

A Check to Be Cashed

*W*hatever I do in my life, I filter it through the knowledge that I am going to be experiencing it again in my life review. Since I have had two near-death experiences and had life reviews during each of them, I feel fairly confident that a life review will happen when I finally die. Knowing that allows me to remember that I am some day going to experience the feeling of the people with whom I come into contact.

By understanding the nature of the life review, I believe that to forgive another person is the same as forgiving yourself. It goes back to the belief that we are all together in a woven fabric of humanity. If you do something out of greed or anger, it will come back to you painfully in your life review. If you are forgiving and loving, the flip side is that it will come back to you, too, most likely in your life review, but most certainly in daily life.

To keep my spiritual ledger balanced, I try to start each day with something spiritual. There are many ways to do this. For me it is with thoughts about the people with whom I work in hospices. Typical of the questions I might have are: Is there anything I can do for them today? Another is, Is there anything I can *learn* from them today?

Many people are not comfortable in hospice work. For me it is a humbling experience to see people going through greater horror than anything I have been through in my life. I have found nothing like frequent exposure to death to make me appreciative of life.

I am all too aware that the next sunset I see may be my last. By reflecting on my life, I have a better notion about who I am spiritually and here on earth.

Chapter 12

DEATH NOT
REQUIRED

S cience and experience have shown us that reflection has the power to heal and transform, to enlighten and humble. Most important, this life review does not have to take place at the end of our lives when we are dying. It can be done at any time during our lives. All we have to do is take a genuine look at ourselves and then make a sincere effort to make changes as we see fit.

I have seen such change made in myself as well as in many people I have met. One of these is a man I will call Rick. I met him in Los Angeles after a workshop that I was conducting. He was in his mid-fifties and could relate to the notion that one does not have to be near death to have a life-changing life review.

"I made a good living from the jewelry store that I owned, but I loved to gamble on the side. I loved it so much that gambling had taken over my life."

Almost every night after work, Rick would frequent one of the illegal gambling halls that he was familiar with, where he would play cards. If he was on a winning streak, Rick would continue to play cards until the early morning. "When I was winning, there was no way I could stop," he told me.

An incident took place after one of these winning streaks that caused Rick to reexamine his life. By his own account, he had won hundreds of dollars playing poker and was exhausted as he left the card room at about three in the morning. As he reached his car in a deserted parking lot, someone approached him from behind and hit him with a blunt object. When Rick woke up, all of his money was missing.

"They not only took my winnings, but also all the money I had from the jewelry store, which I was carrying in a bank bag," he said.

Dazed and hurting from the attack, Rick realized that he was lucky to be alive. Sitting there in the parking lot in the predawn hours, Rick began to review his life. He looked at everything from his childhood to this painful but perceptive moment. There were many things he found positive in his life, but these positives were weighed down by negatives like his obsession with gambling. As he sat on the pavement, he saw the value of everything he had ever done. In this flash of insight, inspired by a hit to the head, he was able to see how much more he could be doing with his life. He vowed to make the positive changes that he felt were necessary.

"This became a moment of perfect clarity for me," said Rick. "I knew that I was ready to evolve as a human being."

Rick continued to work in the jewelry business, but he was no longer found gambling into the night. Rather, he devoted more of his time to his family and to civic organizations that helped people.

"I didn't have to die to get the message," he told me. "All I needed was to have someone slug me and take all the money I had. In a strange way, it was the best thing that ever happened to me."

One of my favorite examples of the healing power of life review, and perhaps one of the best known, comes from the biography of Bill Wilson, the co-founder of Alcoholics Anonymous. He was an alcoholic himself, a heavy drinker who had no control over his savage drinking habit. Even while he was drinking, he considered alcoholism to be a disease of the spirit. Although he struggled with his drinking, both through the medical treatments of the day and by reading philosophy and psychology, Wilson could not cure his drinking habit.

One night he found himself standing at the abyss. Consumed by misery and the cancer of alcoholism, he began to cry. "If there be a God," he screamed, "let Him show Himself!"

What happened next was not a near-death experience, although it has many of the earmarks of one. Wilson had a mystical experience, one that changed his life and the world.

"Suddenly, my room blazed with an indescribably white light," he wrote later. "I was seized with an ecstasy beyond description. Every joy I had known was pale by comparison. The light, the ecstasy—I was conscious of nothing else for a time.

"Then, seen in the mind's eye, there was a mountain. I stood upon its summit, where a great wind blew. A wind, not of air, but of spirit. In great, clean strength, it blew right through me. Then came the blazing thought, 'You are a free man.' I know not at all how long I remained in this state, but finally the light and the ecstasy subsided. I again saw the wall of my room. As I became more quiet, a great peace stole over me, and this was accompanied by a sensation difficult to describe. I became acutely conscious of a Presence which seemed like a veritable sea of living spirit. I lay on the shores of a new world. 'This,' I thought, 'must be the great reality. The God of the preachers. . . .'

"For the first time, I felt that I really belonged. I knew that I was loved and could love in return. I thanked my God, who had given me a glimpse of His absolute self. Even though a pilgrim upon an uncertain highway, I need be concerned no more, for I had glimpsed the great beyond."

This mystical experience brought Wilson into a new state of consciousness. Through a harsh review of his life, he was able to discover a new future. His mystical experience and the life review that led to his personal transformation was the genesis of Alcoholics Anonymous, an organization that gives alcoholics the spiritual foundation to overcome their disease.

*W*hat happened to Bill Wilson was identical in many ways to the life review that occurs during a near-death experience. His was mystical in every sense of the word. The transformation that took place was complete and profound. The main difference was that he did not have to be near death to experience all of the benefits of a near-death experience.

*N*ot all life reviews come with a flash of mysticism or with a bolt of lightning like mine. Many take place over a period of time. Rather than experience an immediate transformation, these conversions take place over a long period of time.

In many ways, the transformations that take a long time are to be more admired than the ones that take place in the blink of an eye. To change over time with no mystical event to inspire such change calls for a great deal of effort. After all, a near-death experience brings a person into a different consciousness almost immediately by giving him a glimpse of a spiritual world that replaces faith with fact. Transformation *without* mystical experience is the spadework of personal spirituality because it calls for the faith that a spiritual world will provide guidance.

A perfect example of this is David Fraijo, a contractor, artist, and lecturer in Phoenix, Arizona, who was introduced to me by my co-author. David was an admitted alcoholic and substance abuser. For David, the cure for a bad hangover was the same thing as its cause, a nice stiff drink. He had spent years as an out-of-control drinker. He drank for fun, he drank for stress relief, he drank because he was angry, and he drank because he was happy. Like others in this lifestyle, his reasons for drinking were irrational. That was okay, though, since he rationalized the irrational.

In his drinking days, David would have said that he had a great relationship with his wife and kids. The reality was that the relationship with his wife and children was based in dysfunction and mistrust. Every member of the family was feeling stress in his own way.

David rationalized his drinking to himself and thought he hid it from his family. When he came home drunk, it was because he'd had a bad day and had just stopped to have a relaxing drink. When he had to throw up in the morning, it was because his allergies were "gagging him," certainly not the hangover it really was. When his wife questioned him about the amount of alcohol he was drinking, he became angry. "I take care of you," he said. "What more do you want?"

Finally, David's wife let him know what she wanted. After his Mother's Day drinking binge, she gave him telephone numbers for two treatment centers and told him to get help. That was in 1986 and is where his life review began.

He looked back over his own family's history and found four generations of dysfunction. He could see that his problems were part of a process that had started many years before.

During the hospital treatment, there were no bright lights or spiritual beings to guide him. All alone, David began the arduous process of change.

"The emotional pain was being purged from me," said David. "What happened was not a breakdown, but an emotional breakout."

He dug backward through his life like an archaeologist. As he did so he uncovered a life made of alcohol, anger, family dysfunction, hurt, and humiliation. He explored his own life and then continued through his family lineage. He could see clearly now that he was not the first alcoholic in his family, just another in a long line of substance abusers.

"I was beginning to realize that this had very little to do with drinking, and a lot to do with my personal history," said David. "I now believe that serious problems are created when people don't own or know their histories."

By arriving at the truth through life review, he began to pursue two goals: To die clean and sober was the first. "I never want to drink or use drugs again," said David. The second goal was to break the chain. "Lies, secrets, shame, ignorance, and fear bestow the disease of addiction to the next generation. Yet it is the life review based in truth, love, and wisdom that will break the old chains. I don't want to pass the disease of alcoholism to my children the way it was passed to me," said David.

David and his family often sit at the dining-room table and review their lives. These informal meetings can range from a discussion of family history to the way one of the children feels about something that just happened yesterday. As a family they are more together than they have ever been, mainly because they have overcome the silence about the issues that secretly controlled their lives. David now sees his problems as spiritual challenges. Instead of believing that there is fear in the future, he now looks forward to its wisdom.

"Truth about your own history is important in overcoming beliefs based in fear and shame," said David. "The bottom line is that if you don't confront your history, it will confront you."

*W*hether through mystical experience or personal reflection, life review can offer deep personal and spiritual change. I won't go so far as to say that an unexamined life is not worth living, but I will say that an examined life is certainly a far richer one. By putting everything else aside and reflecting on our lives from a spiritual point of view, we see ways in which we could have performed better in the past and will perform better in the future.

Through careful and truthful life review, we realize the truth in Nehru's words when he said, "Life is like a game of cards. The hand that is dealt you represents determinism; the way you play it is free will."

I will go one step farther. A Spirit Being might not guide you into your life review, but you will certainly be a *spiritual* being when you are finished.

Through The Centers I have had my own experience in helping people have life reviews.

Ever since the day of my first near-death experience—September 17, 1975—I have been obsessed with the creation of The Centers. These are an object of relentless pursuit for me. As I tell people: "When thirteen Beings of Light tell you to do something, it is hard to say no."

I have never said no, even when I didn't like what they told me to do. I have searched for the methods and material to build the eight components or "rooms" of The Centers. I have also searched for the meaning of each of the components. How do they work? What do they mean? How do they make people realize that they are powerful spiritual beings? And, of course, why was I chosen to build The Centers?

This has all been a great puzzle to me. Fortunately, like all great puzzles, I have slowly figured some of it out.

Some parts are easy, but some are hard, and some may never be figured out. Solving the meaning behind these Centers is a testament to perseverance. There is humor in the spirit world, too, especially when you realize what pranksters the Spirit Beings are. When I reach the end of my rope, they always give me more. I have said that the rope they give me is just to hang myself. I am only kidding when I say that. I know that the rope they give me is to help me find my way. Through them I have learned that discovery is one of the great gifts of life.

In finding my way, I have learned many things. Most important is the realization that we are not poor, pitiful human beings trying to have a spiritual experience, but powerful *spiritual* beings trying to have a spiritual experience. Most of us have just not figured out how to do it yet.

$\mathcal{T}$he first time I put one of The Centers together was in 1977. It was a primitive and piecemeal compilation of the spirit-given elements. I now refer to it as my "Model T" because it seems so ancient compared to The Center I now have. Still, it was a beginning.

One of my goals was to see what effects The Center would have on an alcoholic's drinking habits. Since alcoholism is thought by many to be a disease of the spirit, I reasoned that the information given to me by the Beings of Light might have a lot to do with healing this disease. After all, the purpose of these rooms, as stated by one of the Beings of Light, "is to show people that they can be in control of their lives through God." What better place to start than with people who were out of control?

To test the effects of The Center's system, I treated two friends who had drinking problems. I ran them through the program as I then understood it. The Centers consist of an eight-step program, but I didn't understand then how to put all of the steps together. Still, I did the best that I could.

For instance, the first step involves group therapy. I didn't know exactly how to do this, so I just had the three of us come together and talk.

I realized then that the purpose of this interaction is to loosen up and explore the source of spiritual problems.

I realized, too, that a good dose of humor is extremely important in this regard. When Dr. Raymond Moody compares humor to altered states, he is completely correct. Taking one's life too seriously makes exploration a hard thing to do. Humor cracks much of the veneer with which troubled people surround themselves and allows them to go deeper into their psyches.

Massage is the second step in The Center's program. I didn't understand why massage had any place in a process that was to show us that "we are all mighty spiritual beings." I understand it very clearly, now. Massage helps us break down personal bonds that keep us from self-exploration. It makes us realize that we are all connected to one another in a way that can be extremely beneficial in a physical as well as mental way.

There is something else that happens during massage that I find quite mysterious. Massage has a way of bringing old memories to the surface. I don't know why this happens, only that it does. In these early days, and even now, people recall distant events when they are being massaged. It is almost as though muscle contains memory that is freed when prodded by a masseur's fingers.

After the talking therapy and the massage, I took these two drinkers into the third step, which is sensory deprivation. These days I do this by having people lie on a comfortable couch in a dark room where I use audio and visual techniques to put them into an altered state. Back then I had my two patients sit in comfortable chairs and try to focus on breathing and think about nothing. In the old days I would have them listen to Steven Halpern's music, especially the album *Spectrum Suite,* because it had helped me so much when I was recovering from my lightning strike. The goal of this is to clear the mind, and it is extremely difficult to do. You might try it yourself by just setting this book down and purging your mind of all thoughts. It is not easy, because the mind is active by nature and hard to shut off.

The fourth step is supposed to be hooking clients up to biofeedback equipment so they can see how much control they actually have over their bodily functions. Then I could show them how to lower their blood pressure and make different parts of their body warm or cold. Now, with the advent of brainwave technology, I am on to new frontiers.

The fifth step is to use my intuitive gifts in providing the patients with personal insights. Since I knew these two early patients, I thought psychic interaction would be almost meaningless. I was wrong. After going through the first four steps, things that I had never seen before in these two friends bubbled to the surface. In each of them were family memories that showed why their spirits had been robbed and their self-esteem was so low.

In one case, I could see the patient's father yelling at him in a variety of situations as a child. I could tell that he never felt sure of himself and found that alcohol gave him that confidence that he lacked. The other patient I could see as a boy who felt lost after the death of his father. He was spiritually broken, and beginning in high school he began to drink to fill the void.

The sixth step is the bed. Since 1979 I have built four distinct versions of the bed. If this early Center could be called a Model T, then this first bed was a Mercury spacecraft, the first manned rocket into space.

The basic elements of the advanced versions were present in this bed. The early bed, like the modern one, converted sound to vibration. Still, it was not as comfortable as the modern one is.

I could not do the seventh step with these early patients because I did not understand it then. I really don't understand it now. It called for a surface of polished metal that was shaped in such a way that the person could sit in front of it but not see himself. Since I could not understand the purpose or construction of the device that they showed me, I skipped it in the process with the drinkers. Since the eighth step was a return to the bed, I skipped that too. After all, I reasoned, they were already on the bed, so how could they return?

I had the drinkers go through this process twice a week for about two months. At first it was hard for them to do, as well it should have been since it was so foreign. Then they began to enjoy it. Neither had been so relaxed in years, they said, perhaps ever. After a while they looked forward to the twice-weekly sessions. I learned that the program not only facilitates, but reinforces spiritual behavior.

I found the results to be very interesting. After a couple of months of treatment, one of them greatly curtailed his drinking. He might have had a couple of beers now and then, but it was nothing like the binge drinking he had been so famous for. The other quit drinking altogether and didn't drink again for seven years.

The reason they changed their drinking habits became evident through our conversations. Before treatment they both had nagging anxieties that could be quelled only by alcohol or other substances that dulled the senses. The system has a way of adapting to a person's inner needs. Now they could find a deeper inner peace, a spiritual place that allowed them to get over their craving for alcohol. When they needed inner peace, they could access themselves instead of the bottle.

I am working on improving these techniques. In the future, I hope to develop an even more effective means of dealing with this spirit-destroying disease.

Chapter 13

THE CENTERS

I worked on The Centers for years, but in no way did I have the process figured out. In addition to dealing with my failing health, I was involved in several businesses. In my spare time I tried to put The Centers together as best I could. Even with my best efforts, the steps unfolded in fits and starts.

Then, in 1989, I almost died again. In fact, I hoped I was going to die.

My lightning-damaged heart had deteriorated over the years. Through a cut on my hand, it had become infected. Now I had been told by the emergency room doctor that death would come in forty-five minutes if I did not go to intensive care and begin preparation for valve replacement surgery.

I think he expected me to faint or start crying. What he got instead was a smile as I sat down on the bed. My face was now blue from lack of oxygen, which must have made my smile look even brighter. I could tell that he was puzzled and a little disarmed by my response. Most patients would fear for their lives, but here I was, finding humor in the situation.

As he hovered close to me, I decided to bring some levity into the room. "Well, damn, Doc," I said, still grinning. "Don't you think I ought to lie down?"

What he didn't realize was that I didn't fear death. I had already been dead once. I knew what was in that spiritual land. In many ways I felt the way Christopher Columbus must have when he discovered the new world. He was willing to go home and tell everybody what he had seen. Still, all he really wanted to do was sail back over that great expanse and visit this heavenly place again.

And that is exactly what I planned to do in 1989. I was ready, willing, and happy to be on my deathbed.

The doctors ran tests on my heart and found that the aortic valve was being chewed up by a staph infection that I had picked up through the cut on my hand. Now the valve would no longer seal properly. Every time my heart pumped, a little bit of blood leaked back into my lungs. As a result, I was drowning, a drop at a time, in my own fluids.

If that wasn't bad enough, the antibiotics they were giving me for the staph infection were making me sick.

Still, I was oddly happy. I was going to die, and I was glad of it.

The antibiotics slowed the infection, but the damage was done. As I lay in the bed, I noticed that my lungs rattled with the sound of fluid. The pillow around my head was stained with the blood I was coughing up, and my fingers were a battleship gray and as cold as iron.

"I'm going home," I said to my dad, which was a delicate way of saying that I was going to die. He was horrified. A few years earlier we had lost Mom. Now he could see death approaching one of his sons. I felt sorry for him and my whole family. We were close and loved each other dearly, but still I wanted to leave.

A nurse came in with surgical consent forms for me to sign. They were forms that would allow the surgeons to cut me open and replace my damaged aortic valve with an artificial one. When I refused to sign them, two doctors came in and made their pitch to give me surgery. Still I refused.

"I'm out of here," I told them.

So it would have been if Raymond Moody had not shown up. He had just returned to Augusta, Georgia, from a speaking tour when he had been telephoned by a friend of mine. When she told him I was in the hospital, he promised that he would be there as soon as possible. True to his word, he arrived at the hospital about two hours after receiving her call.

I was convinced that I was going to die. In fact, I

wanted to die. The only loose end that I would leave behind was the completion of The Centers. The Beings of Light told me that I had to have one of the systems completed before 1992. Now, as I lay on what was surely my deathbed, I felt bad that I would fail at my God-given mission.

It was Raymond who changed that.

"You don't have to die," he said. "Stay for me. I need your help."

Had Raymond not said that, I would not be here today. Because he asked me to stay, I signed the forms and was taken to surgery. There I had my second near-death experience. As they put me under with anesthetic, everything became black. Then I left my body and hovered near the ceiling, watching as doctors opened my chest and began their work on my heart.

If ever I have felt mortal, it was when I saw my own heart. Larry McMurtry, the Pulitzer Prize–winning author of *Lonesome Dove*, said that he has never felt the same since having had heart surgery. "I had become an outline, the contents drained out. I think it's because you die during the operation. To this day I wonder where a part of me went after the operation."

As a veteran of heart surgery I agree with McMurtry. A stopped heart is as close as one gets to being dead. Still, I remember where a part of me went during the operation. In my case, I went back to the spirit world.

I went out of my body and watched the surgery.

Then, as before, I went up a tunnel and into a place of bright and brilliant light. I was comfortable there, and I was not surprised by the arrival of a Spirit Being who was with me throughout my life review.

This time I saw my first twenty-five years again, and they were just as miserable and rotten as I had seen them to be before. I was able to contrast those first twenty-five years with my life since the first near-death experience. I saw the people I had helped through my hospice work make their own transition. I was proud to actually feel the difference I had made in people's lives.

The second near-death experience gave me insight into the art of life. As my life passed before me, I could see the good I had done and experience it almost as though it were a sweet fragrance. Little things shown brightly. Instead of feeling fear, anger, and frustration, I felt joy, happiness, and love. There were times, for instance, when I bought somebody a meal, or helped them feel good about themselves. Even though these were brief moments in my life, they were significant and meaningful in this life review. It was obvious to me that all acts of kindness, great or small, carry a great amount of weight in the spiritual world.

After the experience of visiting the other side again, I was glad to come back to the material world. It was now obvious to me that we are in greater control of the world around us than I ever knew. I realized that we could truly change ourselves and, as a result, change the world. I wanted to spread that message. I am glad to be alive, but I have not been the same physically since that surgery. I, too, wonder where a part of me went after the operation, especially the vitality I used to have. I no longer have the same level of stamina, although I try to press on as though nothing happened. One problem of knowing I am a spiritual being is that I ignore my physical body and push it too hard. When I do that, my physical being breaks down and I am dragged down by my own mortality.

Still, I am driven to complete The Centers. One of the first places I landed was at Raymond Moody's home. Since Raymond had asked me to stay to help him, I figured there was a reason. I was right. Raymond was in the midst of a project that would help me figure out The Centers.

Since I first met Raymond in 1976 he has been trying to understand the mysteries of the near-death experience. Part of that has been an attempt to understand how a person can reach the spirit world without having to be dead or near dead. In recent years, he has devoted his practice to understanding the mechanics of spirituality. He has done that at his rural home in Alabama, a place he calls "The Theater of the Mind."

The third floor of Raymond's home is devoted to a "psychomanteum," a facility in which a person attempts to have visionary encounters with departed loved ones. "The wish for reunion with loved ones lost to death is among the most poignant and insistent of human desires," he wrote so eloquently in *Reunions,* his book on the subject. "The desire taunts and saddens us with a litany of *what ifs* and *if onlys,* and mournful pleas for only five minutes more."

When Raymond told me that he was attempting to facilitate visionary encounters with the deceased by using techniques that have been used successfully throughout history, I wondered if The Centers had anything to do with that. After all, grief therapy would be the main reason for having a reunion with a departed loved one. Isn't grief one of the greatest sources of stress for mankind? And isn't stress reduction the main purpose of The Centers?

I decided to pitch in and help Raymond.

I took two models of the bed that the Beings of Light had directed me to make. Among other things, this bed converts tones to vibration and somehow moves through the body's subtle energy fields so that people can relax so deeply they often report out-of-body experiences. Some have even described the vibration as "soul massage." Although The Centers use an eight-step process, not just lying on the bed, I decided that this was the one component that could help Raymond's research the most. I called my apparatus a "Klini" because it looks like the same narrow beds with one end elevated that were used in the healing temples of Asclepios in ancient Greece.

I discovered the temples of Asclepios at Raymond's. In addition to being a medical doctor, he also has a doctorate in philosophy and is a great student of the ancient Greeks. Through his interpretation of Greek culture, I came to understand that many cultures before us have utilized relaxation and biofeedback to create altered states. Through these altered states, ancient man communicated with his unconscious mind and at times possibly the spirit world.

Raymond also introduced me to other facilities, ones called "necromanteums," where people went to make contact with someone who had died. They would spend days, sometimes weeks, in dark caves pondering the memory of the person who had died. If contact was made, it was done by gazing into a polished bronze cauldron at the end of their lengthy stay. Through reading about these places and actually visiting them, Raymond came to the conclusion that a combination of life-review readings, relaxation, sensory deprivation, and gazing into a crystal-clear depth like a mirror could lead to a visionary encounter with a departed loved one.

Not only the ancient Greeks devised such methods of contacting the dead, but other cultures also used the techniques, including the Japanese, East Indian, American Indian, and Chinese; the list of those who used these techniques goes on and on.

Raymond was planning to combine many of their methods and some of his own in an attempt to facilitate visionary encounters.

My purpose in Raymond's psychomanteum project was to use the bed to produce a profound state of relaxation in his study subjects.

Before the patients came to me, Raymond would spend several hours with them talking about the deceased persons they would like to see again. To help prompt their memories and enhance their feelings, he would have them bring photos, paintings, or other mementos. They would first take a relaxing walk, have a light lunch, and then reminisce about the loved one with whom they hoped to make contact.

After reliving his memories with Raymond, the person came to me. I had him lie on the bed while I explained the procedure. First I would get him as deeply relaxed as I could by just talking. When that was accomplished, I put a special device on his head that blocks sound, and turned on the equipment. The subjects felt the tones through the spine. At that point they usually entered an altered state of consciousness by using the sound and tone that emanated from the bed.

When I had relaxed him as deeply as possible, Raymond would take him into a mirrored gazing booth. This dark room had a cushioned chair, a faint light, and a crystal-clear mirror. The subject was told to sit comfortably in the chair and gaze into the clear depth of the mirror. The chair was positioned beneath the mirror and situated in such a way that the subject did not see himself. Rather, he gazed into a clear, dark space.

It was no surprise to me that the study subjects came out of the mirrored gazing booth talking about vivid encounters with their departed loved ones. Some said that they saw loved ones and even had conversations with them. Others felt that they had gone *into* the mirror and spent time with their loved ones in the spirit world. Some said that their loved ones even came out of the mirror and stood with them in the mirror gazing booth.

Among the many conclusions Raymond drew from his work was that these visionary encounters could greatly reduce the pain of grief. I do not want to discuss Raymond's results. He does that better than I can in his book *Reunions: Visionary Encounters with Departed Loved Ones* (Ballantine Books, 1994).

What I do want to discuss is the surprising results that took place on my bed. Even though the bed, or klini, represented only one eighth of The Centers steps, it had a powerful effect on people's psyches, which surprised me. I had expected that the bed would serve only to relax the people who came into the psychomanteum. Instead, it took many of them on the spiritual voyages of their lives.

For example, out-of-body experiences took place in about one of every four people who lay on the klini. I reached the point where I knew when it was happening. The person would be breathing in a rhythmic fashion and then suddenly gasp as though he was having a falling dream. When this happened, I knew that I would hear about an out-of-body experience when the session was over. In many, I heard a lot more.

One case study sums up the results I had at Dr. Moody's psychomanteum:

A woman came from New York to see her late husband. He had been quite sick for several years, which led to severe and unrelenting depression. Finally, he committed suicide.

Their marriage had been a stormy one, and his death left many unresolved dilemmas from their relationship. The woman came to Raymond's facility to solve some of those problems between them and to heal her grief. She thought she could accomplish a resolution by seeing her dead husband again.

She followed Raymond's procedure, spending a long time with him talking about her late husband and looking at photo albums of their time together. This was an extraordinary couple, which was clearly reflected in the joy with which she talked about him and their life.

She and Raymond talked for nearly two hours, and then it was time for her to reach a state of deep relaxation on my klini.

She lay on the bed while I explained the purpose of the klini in Raymond's work. Then I did a life-review reading to help prime her for the experience.

"The goal here is to achieve a state of deep relaxation," I said to her. "This bed will clear your mind and prepare you for the mirrored gazing room."

I told her that some people have out-of-body experiences while on the bed. "If it happens, just relax," I said. "It is quite normal."

I put earphones on her head and had her close her eyes. Then I turned on the music. I could see her muscles relax, and then I could see them relax even more deeply. Her breathing began to slow, and then there was a slight gasp.

She's out of her body, I thought.

I kept her on the bed for more than half an hour before turning it off. When she sat up, the stress was gone from her face. She looked calmly around the room and then began to cry gently.

Raymond and I were baffled as she began to recount the experience she'd had on the bed. First she had left her body. She was sure of this, she said, because she had seen herself from the corner of the room with me sitting next to her, adjusting dials.

Then she felt herself slipping even farther away and was soon in the presence of her late husband. She had a conversation with him about his death. She had taken his suicide personally. After talking to him one more time, she realized that he had been in the kind of pain that no one could help him with. After struggling with mental and physical problems for so long, he decided that the only way out of his pain was to kill himself.

Her reunion didn't stop with her husband. She suddenly found herself in the presence of her late mother. They had the conversation about their relationship that she had longed to have for many years. Their relationship had also been a stormy one. She was able at last to begin to heal the wounds that still existed from those mother-daughter conflicts.

The reunions didn't stop there, either. Still feeling that she was out of her body, she had the sensation of speeding across the country to her daughter's house in Los Angeles. She suddenly found herself standing in the daughter's living room. From her vantage point, she could see the swimming pool water sloshing around. Leading across the patio and into the house was a trail of water that led to the bathroom. She could hear the shower running. In the bedroom she could see a blue skirt and a white blouse laid out on the bed.

And then she came back.

Raymond and I listened with amazement. Then he did a very smart thing. While she was still in a sort of daze, he handed her the telephone and suggested that she call her daughter. She punched in the number and waited. The phone must have rung ten times, and she was just about to hang up when the daughter answered.

She apologized for taking so long to get to the telephone. She had been in the shower, she said, washing the chlorine out of her hair.

"That means you were just swimming," the woman said.

"That's right," said the daughter.

"Then tell me this," said the mother. "Do you have a blue skirt and a white blouse on the bed that you are ready to put on?"

We could hear the daughter talking on the line. She sounded just a little bit angry.

"No, I am not spying on you," said the mother. "I'm in Alabama. You won't believe what just happened to me. . . ."

*A*fter about two years, I decided to leave Raymond's "Theater of the Mind." I had completed my mission up to that point, which was to get a Center in place by 1992. By coming to help Raymond, I had helped create a system of spiritual renewal in the house of the person who had done so much to renew my own spirit.

I could see that our paths were different. He was interested in helping people make contact with departed loved ones. I, on the other hand, wanted to help people face death by having them touch the spiritual realm and know it is there before they die.

I knew that what I had done at Raymond's was the fulfillment of one of the major steps of my vision. I believed that I had been guided there by the Beings of Light as a confidence builder. It worked. My time there helped me answer many of the questions I had about The Centers, and I was grateful to Raymond for the place I had in his work.

It was time to go home and start my own Center.

THE
GUIDING LIGHT

I went home to put together The Centers.

For twenty years I had been following the guidance of the Spirit Beings. For instance, they told me that I had to have a Center in place by 1992. In the years leading up to that date I had no idea how such a Center would happen, but happen it did when I established such a facility at Dr. Moody's "Theater of the Mind."

The next target date that had been given to me by the Spirit Beings was 1997 or 1998. They told me that I was to have a working model completed by then. I don't know why it has to be completed by then, I know only that the Beings of Light have had me on a schedule for twenty years. They haven't led me astray in all that time, so I don't expect that they will lead me astray in the future.

"I am not interested in what the world thinks of my mission," I tell people who criticize me. "I am doing what those Beings of Light want me to do. They keep their word, and I keep mine." Because of commitment, I have approached the project with purpose, focus, and direction.

I began renovating my home in Aiken, South Carolina. It had the perfect history to become the first Center. The house was completed in 1840 by the first licensed pharmacist in South Carolina. He used roots and herbs to make much of his medicine. I have many of his formulas in his note-books that were somehow passed down with the house. Later it became home to two physicians. Now I have turned this old house into a different kind of medical facility, a place that deals with ill-nesses of the spirit.

I was guided in this endeavor by the Beings of Light. In my first near-death experience I was told of the eight-step process that would lead to spiri-tual development. I knew that The Centers had to contain those eight steps.

The environment for The Centers was shown to me in my second near-death experience. In the course of that 1989 experience I was taken to a majestic plateau by a Being of Light. On that plateau was a massive building that looked like a greenhouse. We entered this building, but not through a door. Instead we passed through the glass, a sensation that was like passing through dense fog off the ocean.

The Guiding Light

The fog had all the colors of the rainbow blended into it. It was a colorful potpourri that was scented with every relaxing and heavenly fragrance that could ever come from a garden.

The sources of these colors were the petals of long-stemmed flowers that were in rows down the center of the room. Spirit Beings wearing silver robes tended these flowers, emitting some kind of power that caused the flowers to glow with color as they passed. These colors left the petals and shone through the foglike glass, creating the ever-changing stew of color.

There were tones, feelings, and fragrances that left me feeling relaxed and fulfilled. *What an odd feeling for someone who is either dead or dying,* I thought.

Then the Being of Light chimed in, "This is the feeling you are supposed to create in The Centers," he said. "By creating energies and tones in The Centers, you can make people feel the way you feel right now."

In my own Center I set out to re-create this environment as best I could. I kept in my mind the colors, thoughts, and impressions that I had experienced in this heavenly realm and applied them to the changes I was making in my Center in South Carolina.

I have created seven rooms just as I was told to do by the Spirit Beings. Throughout the house there is stained glass that fills the room with color when sunlight streams through. Biofeedback equipment fills another room, along with a video and music system for state-of-the-art guided imagery and altered states of consciousness therapy. A quiet room filled with comfortable furniture and antiques lets people feel at home so that they can come together in a therapy setting and talk comfortably.

The bed occupies a room by itself.

Some people have expressed concern that The Centers are in some way a denigration of religion. They are anything but that. The Centers are a system, not a religion. They are a process of spiritual exploration, one that can take place without all the dogma of religion. They are a way to reconnect to your true self, and nothing more.

"Think of it this way," I tell the skeptics. "If you don't know who you are in your heart, how can you know which church you belong in?"

*I*n this setting I have worked with clients since completing The Center. My main emphasis is still in dealing with hospice people. I have put a number of them through the program and have always been deeply moved by the results. Hospice patients are usually in pain and are sometimes frightened. After going through The Center's program, the hospice patients I have worked with are always in much less pain and feel less fear. I am not saying that pain and fear disappear. What I am saying is that they are lessened.

I deal with nonhospice patients as well. That is

the way the Spirit Beings wanted it. The mission they gave me on earth was to change people's thought processes by showing them how to rely on their spiritual selves rather than on churches and other institutions.

I could not accomplish that goal if I dealt only with hospice patients. I have to deal with people who are very much alive, as well.

In doing so, I have worked with a variety of people. Some forget how to function as spiritual beings because of all the stress they have in their daily lives. Some have things in their past that they need to confront. Others don't know why they come, but they leave with something anyway.

Here are a couple of those cases.

One day a Japanese journalist came to interview me for a story on near-death experiences. She was a good journalist, pleasant but somewhat removed. She talked to me for a couple of hours about my experience, taking copious notes and interrupting me frequently to get answers that were more specific.

I told her about The Centers and the Spirit Beings who gave me my instructions. She began to write very fast at this point, and I could see that it was of great interest to her. When she found out that there was a Center just out the back door and across the yard she insisted that I take her to see it.

"I will try it if you will let me," she said. "But I warn you, I am not the type who usually is affected by these things."

I had no concern one way or the other. At the very least, the program would put her into a deep state of relaxation. At the very most, she would feel like one of those astronauts in *The Right Stuff*. I told her that I would be glad to have her try the program.

Since she said she had limited time, I did only four steps. We talked for a while about her family and then I gave her a light massage to relax her and help get her accustomed to sensory input. Then I had her lie on the bed and relax even further. As she began to breathe in a rhythmic pattern, I talked to her about the spiritual importance of breath.

"Breathing is the way we communicate with the spirit world," I told her. "It is the only thing that separates us from those on the other side. When you do it consciously and it fully occupies your mind, you can start to touch the spiritual side of life."

When she was ready, I turned on the bed and the other components. I turned the power up slowly and could see her relax even further as the sound began to vibrate throughout her. By the time the bed's energy reached the proper frequency, I could see that she had slipped into a very deep state of relaxation.

When I ended the session about forty-five minutes later, the reporter came awake with a look of bliss on her face. She sat silently on the couch for several minutes to get her thoughts together. Then she told me of her experience.

She had gone into a deep darkness, she said, and felt she was moving very fast. Then she moved past a field of brightly twinkling stars. As she did this, the atmosphere turned a deep blue that faded into gray.

On the other side of this grayness she saw Beings of Light. They had no faces, she said. They just looked like radiant forms of light that lined her way.

Then, looming before her, was a temple that looked like it was constructed of marble. Without hesitation she went inside. There in the middle of the room were Beings of Light, all working intently on a project.

She moved closer to get a look at what they were doing.

What she described was puzzling to me. The Beings were assembling large models that looked like either atoms or universes.

As she sat on the couch recalling the experience, she described these assemblages as "architectural models of the universe."

She was calm as she described her inner journey. At no time did she think this was a dream. "In a dream you have no control," she explained. "Whatever happened here, I could stop and look around at anything I wanted to look at. I was controlling myself just as I am now."

She sat on the couch for a long time. There was a

dazed look in her eyes and a faint smile on her lips. Jokingly I asked if she wanted to go to the hospital.

"No, I want to do that again," she said, pointing to the bed. "I have not been at peace like that in many years."

$\mathcal{T}$he complexities of life unravel in The Center.

This became clear to me one day when a seventy-year-old man came in to "see what would happen."

He explained to me that The Center was not the type of place that he would usually visit. He had little use for self-analysis. But he had recently been diagnosed with cancer and now felt a need to look inward.

I explained the concept of The Center and suggested that stress reduction would at least make him more comfortable. "I don't think anyone goes through more stress than cancer patients," I said.

By the time he went through the program and got onto the bed he was thoroughly relaxed. I left the room for a while and thought he was asleep. When I told him it was time to get up, he insisted that he had not been sleeping, only that he was "in another world."

The first image that came to mind as he lay there on the bed had been that of a flower. He began to get a little annoyed at seeing a flower, but as he looked at it more closely he could see how all the different parts of the flower fit together.

Then as he looked even more closely he could

see that the flower was his own life. He could see his children and his wife and finally himself.

He didn't like the looks of this flower. Especially, though, he didn't like the looks of himself. As he looked even more closely, he could see his life in review.

"It became clear to me that I had changed over the years, and changed in a way that was unpleasant," he told me as he sat on the edge of the bed. "Then I could see just what it was that I didn't like in myself. It was my wife. She had a horrible drinking problem that I always tried to ignore. Instead of having her get help, I denied the problem. When that happened, I started to become more withdrawn. I changed."

He wept as he talked about the ways in which he had changed. His failure to face his wife's alcoholism had forced him to become hard on himself. With changes like that, he had also become hard on his kids. Now, he said, his time was short and he wanted to make life right.

He brought himself around in an interesting way. Rather than go home and declare himself a changed man, he simply changed a little at a time. He devoted more of himself to humor and less to criticism. He decided to change slowly for the good since, as he put it, "I had changed slowly for the bad."

"You don't have to tell everybody you are going to change, that's too much pressure," he said. "You just have to change."

*O*ne day a woman came in not knowing what to expect. She didn't know who she wanted to see or even particularly why she was here. I would normally reject such a client, since I like them to come in with some direction in mind. Since she had been doing hospice work and was exhibiting signs of stress, I let her try the system.

That was fine with me. I talked to her about the system by which The Center works. I told her about the importance of breathing in spiritual communications. I helped her relax and concentrate on breathing so that she could reach a state of deep relaxation. Then I put her on the bed and turned it on. When I brought her back, she told me of an emotionally moving journey.

"My father came to me," she said. "He told me that he was really sorry for what had happened and that he wanted me to know that he was okay."

I was puzzled. "Where's your father?" I asked.

"He committed suicide four years ago," she said. "I haven't even thought about him for two years."

As she processed what had just happened, she began to cry. She knew it was real, she said. She knew other things as well. "I have blamed myself for my father's death because I always thought there was something I should have done to make him happier," she said.

Now she could relax. She had heard from her father's own lips that he took responsibility for what had happened. She had also heard him say that he was happy now, where he had not been happy for many years before he died.

*W*hen I work with hospice patients in The Centers, my goal is to help them have a life review. Some people think it is fruitless to have a life review before they die.

"It can't change my life to have a review," they say. "I am almost ready to die. What good is it?"

My answer is simple. The goal of a life review at the end of a person's life is to evolve as a spiritual being. Even at the bitter end, that evolution is important.

I'll give you an example.

I was at a nursing home when I ran into a sad man whom I'll call Jack. He was in his early seventies, but diabetes had ravaged him so badly that he looked much older than that. He had lost both of his legs to the disease and was experiencing blackouts and heart failure on a regular basis due to the advanced state of his disease.

I convinced the nursing home to let me take him out for a day, and I brought him over to The Center. I told him my story and explained the process of stress reduction to him. Then I put him on the bed and helped him have a life review.

I sat and talked with him for some time. Initially I thought most of his sadness was due to his disease. Most people who are dying face a tremendous amount of depression about their situations. As we talked longer, it became clear that his greatest sorrow was not his illness, but the fact that none of his children would come to see him. Since he had eight children, this meant only one thing to him—he had been a bad father.

At first I thought he must be mistaken. As he talked about his relationship with his children, I had to believe that he had been unusually cruel to his kids.

He talked about whipping his children for little things they did. Sometimes he put them in the closet just to show them who was boss. When he got drunk he was not above beating them for reasons that he could not now recall.

By the time he finished talking about raising his children, I, too, didn't like him very much. Still, I felt that I should help him.

What he relived disturbed him. He saw the foolish and cruel ways in which he had acted. Events came back that he had forgotten. He lived through the eyes of eight children who had no respect for him, and worst of all, had no reason to have respect for him. Now, at the end of his life, he realized that he had passed the hatred he had for his father down to his children. He also knew that they were likely to pass the hatred they had for him down to their children.

"This is the dark side of the cycle of life," I said to him. "Sometimes we become what we hate and then that hatred gets passed down through generations."

Over the next few days I was with Jack as he telephoned each of his children and asked their forgiveness. Some of them came to visit in the next few weeks. Two of them were with him when he died.

Did it help for Jack to have a life review so late in his life? Absolutely. Not only was he able to see the source of his problems clearly, he was able to do something about it and apologize to his children.

To some extent, it prevented the hatred from being passed along, at least with such intensity. It also allowed him to create a "happy ending" to his life. I have no doubt that when he had the life review that began the end of his life here on earth, he relived his attempt to improve his relationship with his children.

It may have been a bittersweet ending, but it beat having no sweetness at all.

The Centers is a story that is twenty years long. It is about peace and fear, life and death, faith and proof. I have flown blind for literally decades, following a message that only I had seen or could hear. Yet I have never been let down by the Beings of Light. They have taken me where they wanted me to go. I have never looked at The Centers as mine, but only as something I was supposed to do.

I think I was given the job of building The Centers because I know what it is like to be afraid, I know what it is like to face death and visit the other side, and most important, I know what it is like to come back and face life again.

The main goal of The Centers is to help those who are facing death. For them, The Centers will create a medium between the spiritual world and this one. Through the program, a dying person can come face-to-face with what they most need to prepare for—death.

For some that might mean having an out-of-body experience and entering new levels of understanding through alternative states of consciousness. For others, it may mean communicating with a loved one who has died and is waiting for them on the other side.

All such experiences decrease the stress of dying and make it easier to let go, especially when there are no other acceptable options.

Another goal of The Centers is caregiving for the caregivers. The aim of this is to reduce stress for those who are helping the dying make their transitions. This includes hospice workers as well as family members. The level of stress on health care workers is enormous. And when I say health care workers, I am not just referring to doctors and nurses. The people who helped me the most when I was hospitalized were the ones who came in and changed my linen or rolled me over when I was paralyzed. They were the ones who talked to me the most and provided me with the most comfort. It is at them that this program is aimed, as well as doctors and nurses.

Now I am at work on a second Center. This one deals specifically with stress management. It will allow people who are feeling deeply stressed by their lives to reattach to their spiritual selves without dogma.

I am building this Center near the Savannah River Project, one of the major nuclear plants in the country and an area that is plagued by stress-related diseases. South Carolina, for instance, has one of the highest heart attack rates of any state in the nation. The federal government acknowledges that people who have the highest levels of stress are people who work at or live near nuclear facilities.

I plan to have this second Center in operation by 1997.

I am excited about finally having a clinic that will be open to the public. I know from thousands of conversations during the last twenty years that The Centers are what many people are looking for. At their very heart, these facilities are nondenominational, spiritual reflection centers. Although this is an eight-step program, it is one that is adapted to the people who use it. This program speaks to each person's needs. Some people go through celestial tunnels, while others see angels. Some just feel enlightened, while others go to ancient places and see things that they never knew even existed.

These Centers give us a chance to separate the mental and physical sides of our lives from the spiritual sides. The program will allow you to dwell in your spiritual self, letting it permeate into your mental and physical life. Once that happens, you begin to explore the spiritual side of yourself in a way that you never have before.

When you realize that there is more to you than what politics, economics, and religion are trying to force you to become, you grow stronger. When that happens, you find the most important truth of all: At the core of all of us is a mighty spiritual being.

Most of us have forgotten that such a core is there. The Centers will help us all remember.

Chapter 15

A DREAM
COME TRUE

*A*round this time I became aware of something else that showed me I was being guided by the Spirit Beings: the office of Alternative Medicine at the National Institutes of Health.

I am a great believer in alternative medicine and have been since I was struck by lightning. Suddenly it appeared as though the largest medical organization in the world was also becoming interested in alternative healing.

My dad introduced me to this type of medicine. The lightning strike had caused excruciating pain down my legs and up my back. My medical records say that the lightning caused "contusions" to my spine. From the way it felt, I would guess that many of the nerves branching from my spine had been severely burned. Nothing short of heavy drugs would relieve the pain.

One day my father came into the house and found me crying. When I told him that the cause was back pain, he helped me to the car and drove me to a chiropractor. It took only one session of spinal manipulation to relieve much of my pain. It was then that I realized that this alternative therapy could do more for me than mainstream painkillers.

Through spinal manipulation I stopped blacking out so often and having massive headaches. Most important, I could get around without experiencing so much pain.

Since then I have dabbled in the so-called alternative therapies. I have tried everything from Chinese herbal medicines to high doses of vitamins, deep muscle massage, and aromatherapy. I have almost always had good results from alternative medicine.

Studying these therapies, I realized that most alternative therapies are very old, some even thousands of years old. Although I am not so naive as to replace Western medicine completely with alternative therapies, I am also not so arrogant as to think that it has nothing to offer. With health like mine, it doesn't hurt to look everywhere for help.

Perhaps what I like best about alternative medicine is the way in which it allows me to take charge of my own health. A famous Chinese physician and good friend, Hong Liu, summed this feeling up nicely. I was getting treatments from him at his clinic in Pasadena, California, when he told me one of the philosophies of traditional Chinese medicine.

"In this kind of medicine, the patient is considered the soldier who fights his illness," he said. "The doctor, by the same analogy, is the commander. I give you the weapons and the marching orders. You fight the war."

Now it seems as though the federal government sees a future in alternative medicine too. This is a huge stride forward. Alternative medicine has always been criticized by mainstream medicine in this country. The creation of a special office to study these "mind/body interventions" was an admission by the medical community that alternative medicine might have something to offer us all.

This new office has another meaning for me as well. The prophetic visions I had during my first near-death experience showed me future wars in Europe, Asia, and the Middle East, to be sure. However, before those battles are fought, there will be a battle for spiritual development that will take place in the health care system. The fight will be over the control of our own health care. It will include battles against technocrats over the right to choose an alternative medical approach. This will be part of a larger attempt to take the rigidity out of managed health care and replace it with humanity.

"The body has a mind of its own and can heal itself," one of the Spirit Beings told me. "People must come to realize that."

The Spirit Beings showed me that within the next nine years, medical science will change so much that much of the equipment now in use will be obsolete. Replacing it will be a new wave of equipment that boosts the natural healing powers of the body.

This equipment will manipulate the subtle energy fields of the body. Some of these energy fields will be strengthened and even directed by electrical current. Others may even be boosted by magnetic energy. In some cases the Spirit Beings showed medicine being taken by a person before the manipulation of these energy fields. The electrical current would then direct the medicine to the site of the illness.

As I have thought about this vision of the future, I am amazed at how similar it is to traditional Chinese medicine, most notably that practice known as Qi Gong, where the Chinese physician uses his energy in combination with herbal remedies to affect the health of the patient.

Also revealed during this vision of future medicine was the role of biofeedback in the treatment of addictions. I saw substance abusers being healed of their addictions through the use of biofeedback technology. This technology shows the healing power of the human spirit by using it to heal a mental and physical disease. I have already accomplished this through the use of The Center technology that was discussed in chapter 12. In the near future, because the future of brain wave technology is advancing at a tremendous rate, the use of such biofeedback equipment to treat addicts will far outstrip my efforts.

If there was an overriding theme in the visions of the future of medicine it was this: We as a people are finally becoming aware of our subtle spiritual bodies. No longer do we view our physical bodies as being separate from our spiritual selves. We now know that the health of our bodies and minds relies heavily upon the health of our spirits too. It is through the subtle energies of the spirit that we can affect the greatest healing.

"If you don't use your spirit to heal," a Spirit Being told me, "then you are not truly healed."

A report from the Office of Alternative Medicine showed me that this knowledge was reaching the highest levels of government. With this report, the battle lines were being drawn.

Much of the *Report of the Panel on Mind/Body Intervention* reads like the outline for The Centers that the Beings of Light gave me in 1975. Just looking at the chapters in the table of contents for the report reads like the instructions for the rooms that I was told to build. Reading portions of what is included in these chapters justified the vision even further. It was as though the NIH were taking the components of The Centers apart and examining each of them individually for its value. Included in the report was proposed research on psychotherapy, meditation, imagery, biofeedback, expressive therapies (like music), therapeutic touch, prayer, and spiritual healing.

The comments that were included in the report could have come from my frequent learning sessions with the Beings of Light.

Comments on psychotherapy were similar in nature to what the Beings of Light told me about group therapy. "Psychiatry should enlarge its concepts of what constitutes appropriate areas for psychiatric intervention," reads the report. "Some of these problems are spiritual and religious in nature, and will require a reexamination of the traditional distinctions psychiatrists have made between psychiatry and religion, and between 'science' and 'spirit.'"

The same was true in what the report said about meditation. "These techniques offer the potential of learning how to live in an increasingly complex and stressful society, while helping to preserve our health in the process."

The comments on prayer and spiritual healing were as radical as can be made by medical doctors in a major government institution. For example: "Until the turn of the century, scientists had no explanation for a very common event: sunshine. An understanding of why the sun shines had to await the development of modern nuclear physics. Of course, the ignorance of scientists did not annul sunlight. Just so, although the evidence is not as immediate, spiritual healing may be valid in the absence of a validating theory."

By reading this report, I knew that what I had discovered years ago was more real today than it was back then. People love and need modern medicine, but they need these natural therapies too. In some way, these therapies come from the organic sides of ourselves and therefore it is virtually impossible to stamp them out. People are trying to go back to nature, they are trying to take control of their lives. In doing so they have encountered alternative methods of healing that have been successful in many cultures for hundreds, even thousands, of years.

The report agreed with this assessment. In its summary, the authors stated my own feelings and the feelings of millions of people:

"We feel that the mind/body interventions described in this report are part of a neglected dimension in health care," the report stated. "They offer people what they are hungry for—a medicine that addresses more than their bodies. In addition to preventing or curing illness, these therapies by and large provide persons [with] the chance to be involved in their own care; to make vital decisions about their own health; to be touched at deep emotional levels; and to be changed psychologically in the process."

*B*efore this report was written, I was asked to be on the ad hoc committee for the formation of the mind/body intervention committee. Our purpose is to examine ways in which to research the effects of the mind on the body. Already research has shown that mind/body intervention significantly reduces medical costs. It has also shown that meditation can reduce cholesterol levels and help reverse coronary artery disease. Other research has shown that something as simple as group therapy can double the survival time of women who have breast cancer that has spread to other parts of their bodies.

It will be our job on the committee to further mind/body research. We will do this in part by looking at methods in which alternative medicine can be studied.

I was asked to join this committee by Dr. Andrew Parffit, a physician with the National Institutes of Health. He had heard about my lectures and knew that I had used alternative therapies in my recovery. He had asked me to speak at the National Institutes of Health on the role of alternative medicine in my life, which I did willingly. Now he wanted me to take a larger role in their search for an understanding of alternative medicine.

Even though I have no medical or scientific credentials, he insisted that I had a place on the committee. "You have been through a lot of medical problems and you have used alternative medicine yourself," he said. "We need people like you to balance the more rational thinkers."

I took that as a compliment. I have not missed a meeting since. One of the first meetings that I attended for the Office of Alternative Medicine was held in Chantilly, Virginia. I can only describe this meeting as wondrous.

A Dream Come True

I moved through a crowd of doctors, psychiatrists, psychologists, hypnotherapists, chiropractors, and herbalists, and realized that the battle over health care had begun. Around me, people discussed the quality of health care and issues such as the right to choose your own physician and type of therapy. They discussed the pros and cons of alternative therapies. Some of the physicians in the room were adamantly opposed to the formation of this new office. They didn't feel as though the federal government should be supportive of medical ideas that didn't fit into the framework of Western medicine. Others were eager to expand their horizons. I listened as one doctor told another that he had spent forty years in medicine and didn't think that Western medicine had all of the answers. He now trusted his instincts when they told him that there were some alternative treatments that could improve quality of care.

As I roamed through this room, I realized that these were people who were truly concerned about the profession of medicine. They sincerely wanted to examine the many ways in which, outside the bureaucracy, healing could be accomplished. Since 45 percent of all Americans use some form of alternative health care, it was obvious to me that the doctors had a groundswell of the population behind them.

Another prophecy had come true. Another sign had been given that I was on the right path. Right there in the hotel lobby I thanked the Spirit

Beings. Once again, I had been helped by their guiding light.

I have no doubt that what has happened at the National Institutes of Health is a message from the Beings of Light. All of a sudden, guidelines for the study of alternative healing are being created within the confines of the federal government. Now, those of us who practice alternative forms of healing are being swept into the mainstream. No longer are we being laughed at by the people in this country who control research. Rather, we are being recognized as having something to offer.

Finally there is recognition that you cannot drug people to health. Thanks to people like Senator Strom Thurmond, a family friend and a great believer in a healthy lifestyle; Senator Tom Harkin; former congressman Berkley Bardell; medical doctors like Larry Dossey, Carl Simonton, and James Gordon; and like-minded health care professionals, all types of healing programs will be studied.

These are people who understand and respect medical freedom. They are not the first in this country. A wise medical doctor said this about our right to choose medical treatments: "Unless we put medical freedom into the Constitution, the time will come when medicine will organize into an undercover dictatorship. To restrict the art of healing to one class of men, and deny equal privilege to others, will be to constitute the Bastille of medical science. All such laws are un-American and despotic." That was said by Dr. Benjamin Rush, patriot, war hero, and one of the signers of the Declaration of Independence.

For me this means that twenty years of struggling to understand what the Beings of Light have been telling me has been worth the effort. Health care is truly where the fight is. There has not been one easy day since I first met the Beings of Light two decades ago. Looking at my notebooks from those times just after the lightning strike, I still see things that make no sense to me. There are rows of numbers, for instance, or phrases that seem to go nowhere but demanded to be written down anyway.

I remember staring for hours at a photograph in an art book of a sarcophagus from early Rome. The photograph showed very ornate coffins that contained the remains of the wealthy or the important. This particular one was a nice piece of work, but I was not admiring the workmanship. There was something about it that I needed to know. I looked at this photograph for what seemed to be forever, although I didn't know exactly what I was looking for. Then I realized that this sarcophagus was shaped like one of the beds I was supposed to make.

Struggling with The Centers has taught me the true meaning of what it is to be spiritual. Through the deep self-examination that happens with The Centers' eight steps, a person is able to find what it is that makes them important. For me it is hospice work. For someone else it may be working with the homeless, helping injured animals, or even coaching Little League. These helpful avocations give a meaning and a value to life. They become as important as making a living because they provide joy and relieve stress.

Stress is often felt when you are not mindful of your true purpose in life. Those true purposes are always spiritual, nonmaterial values that motivate us.

I have come to realize that I am not the only one who has received information about The Centers. During the course of the last twenty years, my path has crossed with many people who have had inspirations that relate to The Centers. It was almost as though the Spirit Beings shotgunned the information to people all around the world and then left us to find each other.

I have talked to people who have had spiritual experiences in which they were instructed to build Centers similar to the one I was instructed to build. I have even talked to people who have developed beds for the same purpose as the one the Spirit Beings indicated to me. In some of the cases, these beds were truly inspired. In other cases, it was just people who were chasing the money.

I spoke to a woman whose husband was dying horribly of cancer. He was a medical doctor, and he knew that his time on earth was not long. Cancer had spread to his liver and other vital tissues and now it was just a matter of time until he died.

He was wracked by his fear of death. In some ways, said his wife, his fear of death was greater than was the agonizing pain of dying.

Early one morning the man awoke his wife to tell her that he was no longer afraid of death. He'd had a vision of the spirit world, he said.

"I know I am going to just walk through a door and come out on the other side," he told his wife. "I am sorry you can't come with me."

He then told her another part of his vision. He had seen places where people could go for spiritual renewal. The best she could remember was that there were a number of rooms in his vision. People would go from room to room and undergo a process in each one. Put together, these rooms led to people being able to touch their spirituality in a way in which they had never touched it before.

In the final days of his life, the doctor hoped to have a more complete vision of this "spiritual hospital." He died without having one, however. She read *Saved by the Light* and contacted me because she wondered if there was any connection between what he had seen and what I had been lucky enough to see and then reproduce.

My answer was yes. I am more convinced than ever that there is a strong and unseen contact between all of humanity. Some Native Americans call this link "the long body," which is the belief that everyone is joined on a sort of spiritual level.

This means that people do not just exist within their own bodies. Rather, there is a link between self and others, or past and present, even life and death. For the Native Americans that meant that the tribe would all exist within the same web of experience for as long as the tribe existed.

The notion of the long body has been used by psychologist William Roll to explain paranormal events like extrasensory perception. For me, it explains many things that have happened in my life, especially my sensitivity to the thoughts of others. It also shines light on the meaning of some verses from I Corinthians:

> *For as the body is one, and hath many members, and all the members of that one body being many, are one body, so also is Christ.*
>
> *And whether one member suffers, all the members suffer with it, or one member be honored, all the members rejoice with it.*

Chapter 16

THE LIGHTNING
SHAMAN

*Y*ou must like the taste of dirt, Dannion, because you always have your foot in your mouth," a friend of mine once said.

I usually deny that, but on this day at the National Institutes of Health in Washington, D.C., it was certainly true.

I was attending a meeting of the advisory board of the NIH Office on Alternative Medicine. During a coffee break a brief discussion of near-death experiences took place. A doctor wanted to know if NDEs had therapeutic value, a question that unleashed an avalanche of opinion on both ends of the spectrum from people standing around him.

For once I was silent on the matter. Maybe it was the high level of education possessed by those around me, or maybe it was just that I wanted to hear what the best and brightest had to say about the subject I knew so well. I was surrounded by people with impressive initials after their names. It was a human sea of M.D.s, Ph.D.s, M.S.W.s, and other degrees, some of which I did not recognize.

As I chatted with a Ph.D. from Maryland, I overheard a conversation behind me. An M.D./Ph.D. from New York was telling a colleague that near-death experiences represented nothing more than temporal lobe seizures caused by oxygen deprivation. These then led to "wishful dreams caused by fear of extinction." I could no longer contain myself. I spoke right up.

"How can you say that?" I demanded. "I've been through two near-death experiences and have seen things in the spiritual realm that I knew were real. I know for a fact that we all have a soul, even though some people doubt it. We all have a spiritual side to balance our mental and physical sides. Some people have just let their spirituality wither, that's all."

The M.D./Ph.D. turned toward me and adjusted his glasses. He looked at my name tag and sneeringly smiled. With the exception of my name, he could see that the tag was empty.

"I failed to get your credentials," he said, clasping his hands together.

I thought a moment. "I am Dannion Brinkley, D.O.A."

*I*f experience provides the best schooling, then you have to believe that I have its toughest degree.

D.O.A. stands for "Dead on Arrival," which is what I have been. Although you won't find a D.O.A. on any university degree, having one does mean that I have a rare form of expertise.

What exactly is the form of this expertise? I have pondered that question for twenty years now without ever coming to a precise conclusion. In a way, for me it has been a search for identity. After all, I am driven to build Centers, but I am driven in such a way that I have to proceed on faith.

I have the spirit-given gift of perception, but it has taken me quite some time to know how this came about and just what it is that I am supposed to do with it. I am still not so sure that this blessing isn't really a curse. Knowing what people are thinking and being able to see their true lives, not just the ones they reveal intentionally, is not always desirable. Being able to glimpse their future is sometimes not pleasant.

And then there are the prophecies. I was shown 117 future events by the Beings of Light that I met during my first near-death experience. In the years since, more than 95 of these events have taken place.

I have become more comfortable with these revelations over the years. They were presented to me by the Beings of Light, who showed me the future in boxes that each of them possessed and that revealed a piece of the world as it would be. These visions have been disturbingly accurate over the years. For example:

- I was shown visions of nuclear destruction that turned out to be the explosion of the Chernobyl nuclear plant near Kiev in the Soviet Union in 1986. I also saw the fall of the Soviet Union and the rise of the Mafia as a form of government.
- In one of the visions I saw an actor with the initials RR winning election to the presidency of the United States. The actor that came to my mind was Robert Redford. The initials were correct, but of course the actor was Ronald Reagan.

Many of my visions concerned the Middle East:

- The war over Kuwait, known as Desert Storm, came to me as images of a great tank battle in which warring armies charged at each other across naked desert. Cannon fire and explosions shook the earth and the date 1990 came into my head. All of that, of course, took place.
- I saw Iran in possession of submarines and nuclear weapons, which I discussed at the beginning of this book. I also saw missiles in the Middle East that were tipped with chemical warheads and were in the possession of radical rulers.

This has all come true since the vision in 1975. A part of the vision that is yet to take place involves a merger of the three main religions— Islam, Judaism, and Christianity—in Israel. The visions revealed that the Catholic Church would successfully establish a Vatican "state-within-the-state" of Israel before the year 2000.

Although the intent of this effort would be a peaceful one, this move would infuriate many Middle Easterners and would lead to war.

◆ In other parts of the world I saw strife. Civil wars in Central and South America led to refugees streaming north to the United States to find a new life. The United States would finally be forced to line our Southern border with the military in order to keep these refugees from entering the country. When that happened, the already strained economy of Mexico would finally collapse.

◆ I also saw a leader from Russia who would speak forcefully about our need to heal the environment. People would rally around him, and the result would be an environmental religion.

Recent events have shown this vision to be true. In 1993, former Soviet president Mikhail Gorbachev formed Green Cross International, an environmental organization aimed at establishing ecological laws and ending pollution.

In 1994, he was joined by religious leaders. They made it official in a bulletin issued by the Environmental Protection Agency.

"The National Religious Partnership of the Environment, which represents one hundred million members of the U.S. denominations, integrate environmental issues into all aspects of religious life. The Partnership represents the U.S. Catholic Council, the National Council of Churches of Christ, the Evangelical Environmental Network and the Coalition on the Environment in Jewish Life."

This tells me that, indeed, an environmental leader has emerged in Russia and is being joined by organized religion.

◆ In the twelfth box I was shown how a computer chip would be developed by a Middle Eastern biological engineer and would be implanted underneath a person's skin and contain all of his personal information. This chip could be used by the government to track a person's movements, and could eventually limit his lifetime by programming the chip to dissolve and kill him with the viral substance from which it was made.

I have yet to hear of dissolvable chips that can kill a person, but the notion of implanted chip technology is everywhere. Some doctors have even recommended implanting such a chip in the breasts of women who have had breast implants. This chip, about the size of a grain of rice, contains medical information about the implant and the patient. Its purpose, doctors say, is to make it easy to follow patients "for a lifetime."

I feel that the right to choose our type of medical therapy—alternative medicine included—can keep these chips from being used.

The Lightning Shaman

It is all amazing to me. Although I saw these 117 future events only one time, I have never forgotten them. Even though I have them written down and stored in a safe place, they are firmly imprinted in my mind. Hardly a day goes by that I don't see hints of these future events in the world around me.

For instance, one need only look at the ethnic fighting between Christians and Muslims in Bosnia to understand why I saw a vision of women in black robes and veils marching through a European city. I now realize that those are Muslim women, forced to fight for their homeland because all of their men have been killed or captured.

I will admit that many of these visions paint a grim picture of the future. The Beings of Light, however, told me something important about these revelations, something that shows the importance of each and every one of us. Here it is:

There is a great spiritual movement afoot on the earth. This is a movement that has the power to change the direction of mankind.

All we have to do is realize that the future is not written in stone. All of the events that I saw in my visions and all of the events that seem to be taking place in the world around us can be altered by group effort. All we have to do, the Beings told me, is view ourselves as spiritual beings, living in a spiritual place, with a spiritual purpose.

The rest will follow.

*S*till I search for just what it is that having a
D.O.A. experience means. Sometimes I stumble
onto some excellent answers.

I recently traveled to Peru with a friend, Abbas
Nadim, where I met a shaman called Rainbow
Bridge. We were in Machu Picchu, the ancient
stone fortress about fifty miles north of Cuzco.
Machu Picchu was the pearl of the Incan empire,
and is thought by some to have been a retreat for
high priests and noblemen of that now extinct
group.

I was completely taken with the setting and
the history of this ancient mystery. Around us
were the sharp green peaks of the Andes
Mountains. These peaks are so high that the thin
atmosphere pulls moisture from their tropical
plants. All day long the mountains ooze wispy
clouds that float heavenward like puffs of smoke.
In a valley at the base of these mystical peaks are
the remains of the last stronghold of the Incan
empire. Having visited Machu Picchu a number
of times, I have little doubt that it was built by
someone who had a near-death experience. For
someone like me who has had two NDEs, it
seemed only natural to compare this sacred site
with the marvelous city of light that I visited
when I was dead. Standing on a peak overlooking
this place of mystery, I knew for certain its creation was divinely inspired.

As we admired this marvel of nature and man,

The Lightning Shaman

Rainbow Bridge said something that gave me insight into myself.

"In my culture, you are a lightning shaman," he said.

I had never heard of such a thing. I asked him just what it meant to be a "lightning shaman."

"My people believe that God chooses people by striking them with lightning," he said. He demonstrated what he meant by picking up a stick and touching me on the arm.

"He does it just like a shepherd chooses a sheep. He reaches out with his rod and touches it. To be touched by God's love, power, and wisdom is the most extraordinary experience that man can ever have."

"It has been an extraordinary experience at that," I agreed.

"Yes, it is the most extraordinary of experiences," he declared. "Think about it. I was chosen by my community to become a shaman and function as the rainbow bridge of my people. I feel blessed to be so chosen. But there is truly something special in people who become lightning shamans. It is a special benediction."

What he said caused me to swell with self-importance. Then he touched me again with the stick and deflated me with his words.

"What has happened to you is special," he said. "In my culture we believe that lightning gives you the power of the puma, the wisdom of the serpent, and the balance of the condor. But you also receive a tremendous responsibility that needs to be accomplished. Otherwise, that wonderful beam of light that God has put into you fades away and disappears."

With that he pulled the stick away from my arm. The mark that it made on my skin remained for a long time.

$\mathcal{I}$ was gratified to hear what he had to say. For twenty years I had been treated like an oddity by medical doctors in my own country. Now I had found a culture that had a name for people like me: lightning shamans.

Through this Peruvian shaman I found a different identity. There were others like me, a whole history of people who had been enlightened by lightning. I was alone in my own country, but here on this mountaintop I had found a category of people with whom I belonged.

As I stood on the edge of this city of stone, questions about my existence flooded my mind. Am I a freak of nature? I wondered. Truly a lightning shaman?

I don't know why I was singled out by that bolt of lightning. I know only that I must not let the light grow dim.

Because of that, my mission is to be continued. . . .

About the Authors

Dannion Brinkley lives in South Carolina, where he does hospice work. He gives more than a hundred talks a year all over the world and is working to establish The Centers that are described in this book.

Paul Perry is the co-author of the widely acclaimed *Closer to the Light* and has written more than ten books on a variety of subjects. Perry was the executive editor of *American Health* magazine and is a former fellow of the prestigious Freedom Forum Foundation at Columbia University.

To contact the authors please write to:
Saved by the Light
P.O. Box 13255
Scottsdale, AZ 85260

The Death and Times of Dannion Brinkley

A Special Video Offer for Our Readers

As a special offer to the readers of *At Peace in the Light,* Dannion Brinkley is offering *The Death and Times of Dannion Brinkley* at a price of only $29.95. That is a savings of $10 off the regular retail price.

This sixty-minute video examines the life of this fascinating man, presenting an intimate look at the world in which he lives.

Directed by award-winning director Marlin Darrah, this video is one of the most timely and pertinent documentaries ever made about the near-death experience.

To take advantage of this special offer, send your name, address, and a check for $29.95 to:

Saved by the Light Productions
P.O. Box 13255
Scottsdale, AZ 85260